STUDIES IN
MODERN HEBREW LITERATURE

GENERAL EDITOR
DAVID PATTERSON

SAUL TSCHERNICHOWSKY

Photograph of Tschernichowsky presented to the author by Isaiah Chernichovsky

SAUL TSCHERNICHOWSKY

Poet of Revolt

BY EISIG SILBERSCHLAG

With Translations by
SHOLOM J. KAHN AND OTHERS

EAST AND WEST LIBRARY

———

CORNELL UNIVERSITY PRESS
ITHACA · NEW YORK

First published 1968

Library of Congress Catalog Card Number: 68–24225

PRINTED IN ENGLAND

Contents

Acknowledgments

THE AUTHOR is grateful to the *American Academy for Jewish Research* for permission to reprint portions of his paper 'Tschernichowsky and Homer'; to *Commentary* for permission to quote sections of his article 'Tschernichowsky: Poet of Myths'; to *Bitzaron* for permission to use parts of his essay 'Saul Tschernichowsky'; to *Hadoar* for permission to quote from his article 'Tschernichowsky and Greek Literature'.

The author is also anxious to acknowledge the courtesy of the National and University Library of Jerusalem for the photostats of a part of the poem *Ani Li Mi-she-li En Kelum* and the letter to Professor Judah L. Magnes, the late President of the Hebrew University of Jerusalem; to the Library of the Hebrew Teachers College of Boston, Massachusetts, for the photostat of the title-page of Tschernichowsky's first book of poems and for the photostat of the beginning of the story about '*David Kahana*'.

The photograph of Tschernichowsky reproduced as frontispiece was given to the author by Isaiah Chernichovsky, a distant relative of the poet. It was taken in 1925.

E.S.

THE PUBLISHERS are grateful to Saul Tschernichowsky's heirs for permission to include translations of some of his poems, and to Mrs J. Slesenger and Miss J. Smith for their help and advice.

The translator wishes to express his thanks to the various publications in whose pages a number of these translations have previously appeared, and with whose permission they are here reprinted. Details of first publication are given in the notes to the poems.

Most of the translations by Sholom J. Kahn have been revised; L. V. Snowman has generously allowed some minor revisions of his versions, and L. Bernard has revised his translation of 'On The Blood'.

Gabriel Preil's virtual collaboration, extending over approximately half the poems included, clarified many obscure points and added many felicitous phrases. Simon Halkin, T. Carmi, Nahum N. Glatzer, Morrison D. Bial, Zevi Scharfstein, Israel Efros, and Reuben Wallenrod have also made helpful suggestions. However, the responsibility for the final versions naturally rests with the translator alone. The translator dedicates his share of this volume to the memories of two former teachers and friends: Yom Tov Hellman and Hillel Bavli.

S.J.K.

Preface

THE TWIN THEME of exile and redemption has inspired countless generations of Hebrew poets from Eliezer Kalir, the early medieval Hebrew poet, to Hayyim Nahman Bialik, the last descendant of a wailing and nostalgic line. It is a bitter-sweet theme, charged with monotony by virtue of endless repetition. Tschernichowsky broke away from the magic circle of aspersion and aspiration. Even linguistically he strayed from early models: the Bible was not the exclusive source of his poetic vocabulary. On a thematic, technical and lingual level Tschernichowsky made a breakthrough. He is the first *modern* Hebrew poet.

His native endowments were massive: they included an epic talent in poetry—a rarity in world literature in general and in Hebrew poetry in particular; a sensitivity to language and a passion for neologism; a literary and scientific curiosity. He used them and was used by them with abandon. His epic gift was responsible for the idylls which were an innovation in Hebrew literature and which can still be considered a major achievement. His literary curiosity was responsible for translations on a grand scale, including the *Iliad* and the *Odyssey* of Homer, the *Symposium* of Plato, *Oedipus Rex* of Sophocles, poems of Anacreon, poems of Horace, two plays of Shakespeare, one play of Molière, poems from English and American, German and French, Finnish and Slav literatures. Scientific curiosity which led him to medicine coloured many of his youthful and mature poems.

His faults were excessive. Since he lacked self-criticism, he did not censure his own banalities of theme and expression; he was less than careful in many important translations; he wrote stories many of which should never have been published and a play which was almost stillborn. Yet the fact remains that he is one of the few great figures in modern Hebrew literature.

Much that is vital in Hebrew poetry today stems from him: thematic innovation, abundance of *genres*, lingual regeneration, variety of form and metric wealth. He stands at the beginning of an era and he is its inaugurator.

PART ONE

Chapter 1

ANCESTRAL MYTHOLOGY AND BIOGRAPHICAL REALITY

THE URBAN CHARACTER of modern Jewry has often been noted by students of Jewish history. The *Shtetl*, the little town, has been one of the main themes of Hebrew literature since 1850. As late as 1930 a contemporary Hebrew novelist Hayyim Hazaz (1898–) could write:

> I love the *Shtetls* of the past—these poor lodging-places of Jews, maligned generation after generation by writers and poets, undermined by versifiers and poetasters, mocked by the stupid and the wise, subjected to governments and governors, invaded by bands of pogrom-makers and robbers till, at last, they ceased to exist and disappeared from the world.[1]

The *Shtetl* was cherished and despised, analyzed with microscopic precision and described with skill. The great reputations of Mendele Moher Sefarim and Shalom Aleihem rest on their portraiture of the *Shtetl*. Tschernichowsky, a rural Jew, is the first singer of rural life in modern Hebrew literature. He spent his formative years of childhood and adolescence in the village of Mikhailovka—on the borderlands of the Ukraine and the Crimea. And he maintained an abiding love for his birthplace. Indeed, the landscapes in many of his poems are transformations-in-verse of his birthplace. In his idyll *Berit Milah* (Circumcision) the village of Bilobirka is really Belozorka near Mikhailovka. In one of his later idylls, *Hatunatah Shel Elkah* (Elka's Wedding) he mentions his native village by name—a large and populated village, 'heavy with good wheat'. And it is, perhaps, not without interest that the name of his

---

1. See the opening paragraph of the story *Dorot Ri'shonim* by Hayyim Hazaz in *Sippurim Nibḥarim*, Tel-Aviv, 1952, p. 7.

grandmother was Elka. The entire idyll—the longest and best of his efforts in that *genre*—may be regarded as a paean in praise of Mikhailovka, its fields, its fruit and its people.

Born on the twentieth of August in 1875,[2] Tschernichowsky spent the first fifteen years of his life in his native village. The vistas of southern Russia became part and parcel of his poetic personality. It may be said without exaggeration that the landscape of southern Russia permeated the mind of Tschernichowsky.

Throughout his life he was rightly regarded as a handsome man. He was tall, robust and massive. His thick unruly hair and his generous moustache added a slight touch of quaintness to his appearance. Men—and especially women—often turned around to look at his striking figure. This poet with classical tastes and predilections was in looks, at least, the personification of the Byronic type, the romantic man *par excellence*.

The ancestors of the poet originated in Tschernichow in the Ukraine: hence the name. In an autobiographical sketch Tschernichowsky made much of his family mythology[3] and vaunted the health, the strength, the longevity of his forefathers. His grandfather's brother lived to be more than 113 years old and celebrated his second *Bar Miẓvah*. Another ancestor saved his life by sheer sang-froid during the massacres by the Cossacks in 1768. He hid in a haystack and uttered no cry of pain when the spear of a Ukrainian ruffian pierced his foot. A third ancestor was in the army of Nicholas I when it endeavoured to quell the Hungarian revolution of 1848. At the end of a long life the latter became a true disciple of Tolstoy, a pacifist and a vegetarian. Tschernichowsky used his immediate forefathers as characters in numerous poems. In 'Elka's Wed-

2. The date is authenticated by the poet himself in response to a questionnaire sent out by the literary archives—*Genazim*. It was published on the twentieth anniversary of his death. See *Genazim* 13–14, 1963, p. 5.

3. 'The mythology of our family' —this is the phrase used by Tschernichowsky in his 'Autobiography', *Ha-Shiloaḥ* XXXV, 1918, p. 97.

ding' he mentioned the maternal, 'half-heretic' grandfather, Saul Karp who had wandered as far as Turkey and who knew several languages—Italian, French, Ukrainian. Only two years before his death, he glorified him in two poems: *Saba Maflig le-Odessa* (Grandfather Sails to Odessa) and *'Al Tel ha-'Arabah* (On a Hill in the Plain). In 'Grandfather Sails to Odessa' he described—not without humour and verve—an adventurous trip undertaken by his ancestor with a Ukrainian friend in a sailing boat. For his grandfather had lived in *Golaya Pristan* (Hollow Harbour) and felt an affinity with water. His signet ring, with the engraved two carps, symbolized his name Karp and the month of his birth under the zodiacal sign of *Pisces* (Fish).

But Tschernichowsky was not merely describing an odd journey by an odd grandfather. Always on the alert for genealogical mythology, he somehow connected the ancestral urge with the Hebrew sailors of biblical times who lived by the shores of Ezion-geber[4] (modern Eilat) and who sailed with Phoenicians to Ophir and other far-away places. The fusion of private and public myth was as characteristic of Tschernichowsky as the fusion of the private and public self in the biblical psalms.

'On a Hill in the Plain' is an idyllic description of a village where the poet's grandfather spent most of the last years of his life. It is a perfect counterbalance to the dynamic poem 'Grandfather Sails to Odessa', a static representation of the earth and the fulness thereof. As one reads it, one can almost smell the waving wheat and almost hear the hooting owl. In this poem, too, Tschernichowsky coupled his private mythology with ancient backgrounds in the description of the mound where bones of warriors were found or where a golden diadem, made by a Greek artist, was unearthed. And with that surprising

4. Ezion-geber is mentioned seven times in the Bible: as a station in the Exodus of the Jews from Egypt (Numbers 33:35, 36; Deuteronomy 2:8); as a shipbuilding locality of King Solomon and King Jehoshaphat as well as a place visited by King Solomon (1 Kings 9:26; 22:49; 2 Chronicles 8:17; 20:36).

suddenness which is the glory of poetry and the despair of its critics, the poet turns to his mother:

> Mother, dear mother, what crown of all possible crowns
> have you fashioned for me?
> Oh, it was not a crown of pure gold and it was not a chaplet
> of flowers.
> It was the laurel framed in nettle and nettlewort.

This is not senile self-pity, but rather the reflection of a mature mind toward the end of his life. The poet is, after all, a crowned individual. The durable plant of Apollo's servants, the laurel, is his distinguishing mark; and so is the garland of thorns.

Tschernichowsky also dedicated a poem to his great-grandmother and described her work as a midwife. She had no diploma and no official license. But she served for the love of service and she assisted the poor with preferential care. The poet's father was also depicted with almost objective respect in one of the last poems. In his youth he went from fair to fair to peddle his wares. By sheer accident he acquired the healing art of the veterinarian which he practised without charge, to the great delight of his neighbours. Tschernichowsky who was a physician by profession learned his first lessons in medical lore from his father and from familial reminiscences.

Both outstanding Hebrew poets of the twentieth century—Bialik and Tschernichowsky—reminisced in poetry about their respective family backgrounds toward the end of their lives: Bialik in his excellent four-part poem entitled *Yatmut* (Orphanhood), Tschernichowsky in a series of poems about his parents, his grandparents and his great-grandmother. Both were in search of the lost Eden of childhood, both had devised their own mixture of *Dichtung und Wahrheit*. Bialik was able to orchestrate his own and his people's childhood in such verbal symphonies as *Megillat ha-Esh* (The Scroll of Fire), *Ha-Matmid* (The Ever-diligent), and *Mete Midbar* (The Dead of the Desert). In 'The Dead of the Desert' Bialik rediscovered the childhood of his people, in 'The Ever-diligent' he retraced his youth, and in

חזיונות ומנגינות

שירים.

מאת

שאול טשרניחובסקי

הוצאת „תושיה".

וואַרשא. תרנ"ט.
בדפוס מ. י. האַלטער ושותפו, נאַלעװקי 7.

XEЗIОНОТЪ УМАНГИНОТЪ

т. е.

Видѣнія и Пѣсни.

Стихотворенія С. Черниховскаго.

Изданіе „Т У Ш I Я."

ВАРШАВА. 1898.
Тип. М. И. Гальтера и Комп., Налевки 7.

Title-page of Tschernichowsky's first volume of verse *Hezyonot u–Manginot* in the Library of the Hebrew Teachers College, Brookline, Massachusetts

'The Scroll of Fire' he fused the two phases of childhood darkly and enigmatically. Tschernichowsky sought to create a family myth and place it in the context of ancient mythology. The family poems—'Elka's Wedding', most of the idylls and the poems on Saul—are poetic glorifications of a private past and a public past which reach to the roots of the human race, and not only to the roots of Judaism as in the poetry of Bialik.

Tschernichowsky's parents seem to have differed in temperament and inclination. The father was a store-keeper, simple to the point of naïveté, honest to a fault, neither fanatic nor heterodox. The mother was clever and convivial, poetic, a lover of flowers and a lover of songs, almost a modern woman. And an aunt—his mother's sister—was one of the first Jewish students in Russia. But the poet's home was traditional though not rigidly orthodox. The commandments were observed with joy, the holidays were high points in the uneventful calendar of the village year.

At five Tschernichowsky was tutored in Russian by his aunt, at seven in Hebrew by his father. A private teacher was hired for him and a few other children in the village. And the boy acquired Hebrew through translation into Russian, the knowledge of the Pentateuch without *Leviticus*. That was a revolutionary method in educational practice. For *Leviticus* had been the beginning of biblical learning for the Jewish child, and translation into Yiddish the acceptable way of study for centuries.

When Tschernichowsky was nine years old, two Hebrew teachers came to Mikhailovka and taught the youngsters to love the language, the literature, and the land of Israel. The future poet was their star pupil. What he learned was not, perhaps, most suitable from the educational point of view: the turgid and slanted tracts of Jewish history, biblical and rabbinic lore by Isaac Ber Levinsohn (1788–1860), the romantic novels of Mapu (1808–1867), Grace Aguilar's *Vale of Cedars* in a Hebrew translation, a little Talmud and a lot of the aggadic miscellany of the sixteenth century *'En Ya'aḳob (The Fountain of Jacob)*.

In the course of time private instruction was supplemented

by systematic schooling. Since there was no boys' school in Mikhailovka, Tschernichowsky became a pupil in a girls' school where he was one of the only two boys. There he learned Russian and German, natural sciences and mathematics, history and geography. He also became an avid reader. The books of Verne, Dumas père and Eugène Sue, the *Iliad* and the *Odyssey*, *Robinson Crusoe*, *Hamlet* and *Macbeth* fascinated him in their Russian translations. *Macbeth* made a particularly strong impression on the future translator.

Tschernichowsky was barely ten when he received the poems of Micah Joseph Lebensohn (1828–1852) as a gift from his Hebrew tutor. The impact was instantaneous. The epic vistas, musical grace and lightness of touch of Lebensohn's poetry appear to have fascinated Tschernichowsky and nourished his dormant talents. At twelve he composed a play which was lost and a poem on Uriah the Hittite who was so unjustly used by David. And he also longed in his early youth to be as good a poet as Aaron Elijah Pompiansky, the imitator and plagiarist of Goethe.

It is not without interest that the boy Tschernichowsky compiled a Russian–Hebrew dictionary. He had dabbled in translations and decided, rightly, that Joshua Steinberg's dictionary was highly inadequate. In later life he was to pioneer terminology in the *Dictionary of Medicine and Allied Sciences* which he compiled and edited together with Dr. A. M. Masie (Jerusalem, 1934). Of other early and non-extant 'works' a novel with an eastern background and a history of the Jews should be noted. The boy was groping for a literary medium but had not yet discovered his latent talent for poetry. But his affinity with the Greeks was marked. The *Pentateuch*, in his youthful estimation, was an epic like the *Odyssey*. Even the girls of the village, in curious prescience, called him 'the salted Greek'[5]—an allusion to his strangeness and to the mercantile

5. *Soleny Grek* in Russian. At that time Greeks were the purveyors of salt from the Crimea to the cities of Southern Russia. See Joseph Klaus-ner, *Sha'ul Tschernichowsky: Ha-Adam we-ha-Meshorer*, Jerusalem, 1947, p. 12; *Ha-Shiloah* XXV, 1911, p. 266; *ibid.*, XXXV, 1918, p. 99.

pursuits of Greeks in Southern Russia. That the child Tschernichowsky was father of the man Tschernichowsky was true in
more ways than one. Most of his inclinations and attitudes
manifested themselves in early life: his variety of literary interests, his scientific bent, his universalism, his love of the
Greeks, his pride of ancestry. Only his main endowment—the
gift of poetry—still lay dormant. It needed stimulation from
and contact with a metropolitan centre. And it surfaced in
Odessa—the city which was known as 'The Southern Belle'.

Tschernichowsky was fifteen when he entered the private
High School of Commerce which was under the supervision
of Hayyim Hochman[6] in Odessa. The two years of formal
instruction, 1890–1892, spent under the tutelage of learned and
not-so-learned men, were less important than the Hebrew
literary milieu. In the last decade of the nineteenth century
Odessa became the chief centre of the Hebrew renaissance. The
budding talents of Ahad Ha'am, the ideologue of Zionism, and
Bialik its poet laureate, Nahum Slouschz, Joseph Klausner and
Simon Dubnow, the well-known scholars, were welcomed by
their elder contemporaries—Mendele Moher Sefarim, the
novelist, and Moses Leb Lilienblum, one of the last of the
'Enlightened' and one of the first proto-Zionists who were
known as Lovers of Zion (Ḥobebe Ẓiyyon). A host of lesser luminaries who contributed to Odessa's Hebrew annuals like Pardes
and miscellanies such as Kawweret enlivened the atmosphere of
the city. It was a heady and exhilarating experience to be a young
man of letters in Odessa at that time.

An important event in Tschernichowsky's biography—
though not in his poetic development—was his meeting with
Klausner in Odessa. They became firm friends, and remained
friends throughout their lives,[7] in spite of their differences in

6. Tschernichowsky devoted an
excellent essay to Hochman, 'the
only Jewish professor' at the time,
the uncompromising Jew, the neglected idealist who struggled to make
a poor living out of a poor school

and finally ended in an asylum. See
Kitbe Sha'ul Tschernichowsky VII,
Tel-Aviv, 1932, pp. 200–5.

7. As early as 1895, on a short
visit from Odessa to his native
village, Tschernichowsky addresses

talent and temperament. Klausner was the slow and deliberate scholar, the voracious reader and the prolific writer, the zealous Zionist and the ardent though less than brilliant critic of Hebrew literature. Tschernichowsky was the creative poet in search of his own identity and in pursuit of *joie de vivre*. Klausner, then, was a minor event in the inner biography of the poet: he guided Tschernichowsky in his reading, introduced him to Hebrew literary circles and fortified him in his resolve to become a Hebrew poet. But Tschernichowsky maintained a life-long attachment to his scholarly friend and dedicated to him his fine poem *Taba'at Lo la-Adonai* (God's Ring) which was written in 1935. On the other hand, the poet remained a major force in Klausner's life. The scholar was fascinated by his abilities and paved the way for his recognition. Throughout his life Klausner delved into the mystery that was Tschernichowsky, in a host of articles and in a good biographical study of the poet who was neither the proverbial ingrate nor the fawning sycophant, but who accepted the admiration of his friend and critic with unaffected spontaneity.

It was Klausner who sent the first two poems by Tschernichowsky to Hebrew editors: one *Ba-Ḥalomi* (In my Dream) which appeared in the American–Hebrew periodical *Ha-Pisgah* under the editorship of Wolf Schur on December 9, 1892[8] in Baltimore, and one *Massat Nafshi* (My Ideal) which appeared

---

Klausner as 'my friend, my loved one'. See an unpublished letter of April 2, 1895 from Tschernichowsky to Klausner in the Manuscript Collection of the National and University Library of Jerusalem.

8. The date for the publication of the first poem by Tschernichowsky is December 9, 1892, not December 16, 1892 as given incorrectly by Klausner in his book *Sha'ul Tschernichowsky*, p. 24, note 2. *Ha-Pisgah* where the poem was published lasted ten years (1889–1899) and boasted on its masthead in quaint English that 'it is the chief organ of the Jewish clergy and of the most intelligent class of Israelites in America.' But, in point of fact, it imitated the worst features of Hebrew periodicals in Russia—*Ha-Maggid* and *Ha-Meliẓ*—and it never rose above undistinguished reportage in undistinguished language. On the state of Hebrew letters in America at the end of the nineteenth century, see Eisig

in *Ha-Sharon* under the editorship of Gershom Bader and Menahem Mendel Malles in Cracow, Galicia, in 1893.

Neither the periodicals nor the teenage poet's poems showed any distinction. As a matter of fact 'In My Dream' was never re-published in any collection of Tschernichowsky's poems. In tone and in technique it harked back to the period of enlightenment. The sentimental dirge, cast in seven six-line stanzas, produced an effect of utter monotony.[9] The content, reminiscent of a medieval lament over Zion, was as hackneyed as other elegiac wailings of similar ilk: in a dream, in the stillness of the Palestinian night, the nightingale sings about the people that once dwelled in Zion but now wanders all over the globe. The poet is saddened by the song, and even the buds and flowers, the palms and the olives seem to be affected by the wailing nightingale. It is a curious coincidence that the great contemporary of Tschernichowsky, Hayyim Nahman Bialik, also used a conventionalized bird to convey his sentimentalized yearning for Zion in his first published ode *El ha-Zippor* (To the Bird).

Under Klausner's influence Tschernichowsky began writing in Hebrew exclusively and abandoned any ambition he may have had to write poetry in Russian. Later in life he even withstood the temptation of very lucrative offers to write poetry in Russian and publish it in the Russian language Zionist weekly *Razsvet*. Only a few articles in Russian survive from his pen, and these were written to satisfy a financial rather than a psychological need.

Silberschlag, 'Hebrew Literature in America: Record and Interpretation,' *Jewish Quarterly Review* XLV, April, 1955, pp. 418–23; *idem*, 'Development and Decline of Hebrew letters in the United States' in *The American Jew: A Reappraisal*, ed. Oscar I. Janowsky, Philadelphia, 1964, pp. 177–81.

9. On prosodic drabness in the period of enlightenment see Eisig Silberschlag, 'Parapoetic Attitudes and Values in Early Nineteenth-Century Hebrew Poetry', *Studies and Texts II*, ed. Alexander Altmann, Harvard University Press, Cambridge, Massachusetts, 1964, pp. 118–119.

Tschernichowsky's poem 'My Ideal' was favourably noticed in *Ha-Meliz*, the most important weekly of the time, by the influential critic Reuben Brainin, who wrote a few years later, in 1898, a glowing introduction to Tschernichowsky's first book of poems, *Ḥezyonot u-Manginot* (*Visions and Melodies*). Nevertheless, Tschernichowsky experienced difficulty in publishing his poems, of which there were always many in the drawer, but few in the literary publications. He had to place them in out-of-the-way journals for editors were not hospitable to the new and strange poet.

After leaving the private High School of Commerce in 1892, Tschernichowsky passed the entrance examinations to the public High School of Commerce in 1893 and studied there for the next three years. It was in that school that he acquired a certain fluency in German and English, French and Italian. An avid and creative reader, he knew how to utilize his newly acquired knowledge. In those years he translated Shelley's 'The Cloud', Burns' 'John Barleycorn' and 'My Heart's in the Highlands', Longfellow's 'Excelsior' and *Hiawatha*. The American poet whose reputation has suffered a serious decline since the end of the nineteenth century, appealed to the Hebrew poet, who also translated his *Evangeline*.

During the last years of the nineteenth century Tschernichowsky wrote the poems which were inspired—*mirabile dictu* —by a Greek girl, Maria Valiano. Several poems were dedicated to her: *Le-Miriam* (To Miriam)—a hebraized form of her Christian name—and the Heinesque poem which begins with the line:

I will carry your name on wings of song.[10]

What is, perhaps, equally important: the poet's attraction to all things Greek was strengthened by a living symbol of Greek beauty. Since Greek and Latin were not taught in the High School of Commerce, he studied them privately—out of

10. See Heine's famous poem which begins with the well-known lines: Auf Flügeln des Gesanges, Herzliebchen, trag ich dich fort.

necessity as well as love, for he had to know the classical languages in order to pass his entrance examination to the university. In later years he inaugurated a new era in Hebrew translations from the classics. It may be said in his praise that he is the father of Greek literature in Hebrew garb.[11]

But Tschernichowsky was not unaffected by the historic events in Jewish life. The birth of the Zionist movement in the last years of the nineteenth century inspired such nationalist poems as *Be-Lel Ḥanukkah* (On Hanukkah Night) and *Se'u Nes Ẓiyyonah* (Carry the Banner to Zion). It was only right that he should compose a poem which carried the Zionist flag in its title for he was the honorary secretary of a Zionist organization by the name *Nes Ẓiyyonah*.[12] Tschernichowsky's Zionism was neither militant nor strident: it was primarily a matter of self-identification. He visited and admired the non-Zionist Mendele Moher Sefarim for his brilliant portraiture of Russian Jewry. He even wrote a reminiscent feuilleton about the grand old man of Hebrew letters.[13] And he was to dedicate to him in later life one of his best nature poems *Ḳisme Ya'ar* (Charms of the Forest).

The first collection of Tschernichowsky's poems—*Visions and Melodies*—appeared at the end of 1898 in Warsaw. It was a slim volume of 86 pages, prefaced by Brainin and recommended to the publisher Ben Avigdor by Klausner and another youthful friend of the poet, Asher Segal. No one—except the prefacer—

---

11. On Tschernichowsky's translations in general see F. Lachower, *Tschernichowsky be-Targumaw*, *Mo'-znayim*, 1935, pp. 560–70; on Tschernichowsky's translations from the Greek see Eisig Silberschlag, 'Tschernichowsky and Homer', *Proceedings of the American Academy for Jewish Research* XIV, 1944, pp. 253–265.

12. There were at the time two basic Zionist organizations in Odessa: *Bene Ẓiyyon* and *Nes Ẓiyyonah*.

See Saul Tschernichowsky, 'Ha-Kontrabandistim be-Odessa', *Ha-'Olam*, July 16, 1926, p. 557; *idem*, 'Ha-Studentim', *Ha-'Olam*, October 12, 1928, p. 780; *idem Yiẓḥaḳ Yoel Linetzki*, *Ha-'Olam*, December 7, 1928, p. 930 and *Kitbe Sha'ul Tschernischowsky* VII, pp. 157–68.

13. See Saul Tschernichowsky, 'Mendele Moher Sefarim', *Kitbe Sha'ul Tschernichowsky* VII, Tel-Aviv, 1932, pp. 211–15.

sensed or said that a literary event had taken place. On the contrary, J. H. Ravnitzky, the critic and literary 'partner' of Bialik, blasted Tschernichowsky's poems in the most influential literary monthly *Ha-Shiloaḥ*. He complained about the poet's poverty of language, meagre knowledge of Hebrew, and above all, poverty of theme. Brainin exaggerated, according to Ravnitzky, the worth of Tschernichowsky's poems: they lacked originality and seemed to be mere translations of other poets. 'You will not find in these poems a wealth of new feelings. And needless to say, they have not many new thoughts. . . . Most of them describe springtime, the loveliness of flowers (almost always roses), the chirping of birds (almost always the nightingale and the swallow), the eyes of the beloved and the fire of desire.' The only good thing Ravnitzky had to say about Tschernichowsky was that 'sometimes he can depict some nature scenes in clear and precise colours'. He also granted him a 'gently sounding voice and a certain beauty'.[14] But on the whole he was derogatory and deprecating. For Brainin had, perhaps unwisely, juxtaposed the solid achievements of Judah Leb Gordon with the green *élan* of a young poet. And Ravnitzky was defending conservatism against avantgardism in literature. It was zeal turned to myopia. In extenuation and expiation of Ravnitzky's literary sin it should be noted that, in 1914, he published a large volume of Tschernichowsky's poems under the imprint of *Moriyyah* which was managed jointly by Bialik and himself.

The Hebrew public and the critics were not quite ready for Tschernichowsky: his preoccupation with love, his peculiar prosody and his non-biblical language were qualities that tended to alienate the poet from his readers. Then again, the sixty poems in the first volume—46 original and 14 translated from Greek, German, French, Russian and English—seemed too slight, too trivial, too unchallenging for his contemporaries. Worse than that: they offered no lingual pyrotechnics, no puns, no artificial combinations of biblical half-verses and repetitive

14. See *Ha-Shiloaḥ* VI, Berlin, 1899, pp. 260–1.

rhyme-schemes such as delighted the literary audience at the end of the last century. A serious reader and writer like Ahad Ha'am would not accept a poem for an annual which he edited, the *Luah Ahiasaf* for 1897, because the poet wrote—*horribile dictu*:

> I shall embrace you, love, and kiss you
> With passion and with fire.[15]

On the other hand, Moses Leb Lilienblum, a precursor of Zionism and an important figure in Hebrew literature at the end of the nineteenth century, refused to accept Tscherni-chowsky's poem *Me-Hezyonot Nebi' ha-Sheker* (From the Visions of a False Prophet) because it began with the biblical phrase: 'The Word of God came to me.' He justified his rejection with the haughty sentence (in Russian): 'I do not believe that God speaks to Tschernichowsky.'[16]

Few, all too few, noticed that even close reading failed to exhaust the poetic worth and strength of *Visions and Melodies*. One of the few was Klausner who wrote the first of his eleven essays on Tschernichowsky;[17] the other was Abraham Jacob Paperna who, unlike Ravnitzky, admired Tschernichowsky's originality and style. But even Paperna could not help pointing out Tschernichowsky's grammatical, rhyming and rhythmic errors. And in a patronizing tone he declared:

'The poetry of Mr. Tschernichowsky is beautiful and pleasant, but still young and tender; its flowers are fresh and full of colour, but they have not yet developed sufficiently . . . workmanship and polish are lacking in a number of these poems. In some of them we feel a lack of logical coherence, in others— fuzziness of thought, unclear imagery'.[18] But he concluded

15. The poem appeared under the title '*Al Kanfe Dimyoni*, in Tscherni-chowsky's first book of poems *Hezyonot u-Manginot*, Warsaw, 1898, pp. 36-7.

16. See Saul Tschernichowsky, 'Moses Leb Lilienblum', *Ha-'Olam*' November 2, 1928, p. 841.

17. They appeared in collective form in Klausner, *Yozerim u-Bonim* II, Jerusalem-Tel-Aviv, 1929.

18. See *Sefer ha-Shanah* ed. Nahum Sokolov, Warsaw, 1900, pp. 257-8.

that 'even in verses which lack perfection, the sensitive and understanding reader will see the hand of a wonderful artist and the spirit of a poet touched by the spirit of God.'[19]

The fact that Paperna devoted nine long pages to a newcomer and adorned his review with copious citations from the poet, shows the esteem the elder critic conceived for the budding poet.

What was to distinguish Tschernichowsky from his fellow poets in the future was immediately apparent in the first volume: a wealth of *genres*—sonnet, ballad, idyll; love of translation; dedication to the national ideal in non-jingoistic stance; incorrigible optimism; belief in gradual progress; and, above all, a lapidary form of expression—not sweet, not charming, but tensile and expansive. Even his faults were apparent in the first volume: the awkward and drab phrasing in the longer poems, a clarity verging dangerously on the obvious, a total lack of mystery.

Tschernichowsky spent the next few years of his life, from 1899 to 1903, in Heidelberg where he studied medicine. He also attended Kuno Fischer's lectures on philosophy and on Goethe's *Faust*.[20] He read the German classics—especially Goethe—and translated Goethe's greatest lyric

Über allen Gipfeln
Ist Ruh . . .

Although he revised the translation many times, he remained as unsuccessful as other translators of the lyric in Hebrew or in other languages: the extreme economy of words in a compact rhyme-scheme eluded—and still eludes—the most competent of translators. He did well, on the other hand, by the German

---

19. *Ibid.*, p. 262.

20. Ernst Kuno Berthold Fischer (1824–1907) was one of the brilliant historians of modern philosophy and a sensitive critic of German literature. His lectures at the University of Heidelberg where he served as professor of philosophy from 1872 were very popular with the more earnest students. See Klausner's autobiography, *Darki Likra't ha-Tehiyyah we-ha-Ge'ulah* I, Tel-Aviv, 1955, pp. 97–8.

poet's *Römische Elegien* (*Roman Elegies*) and, especially, his epic *Reineke Fuchs* (*Reineke the Fox*).

Heidelberg—the picture postcard city with its student-prince atmosphere—fascinated the poet. He loved the old university which had been founded in 1386 by Elector Rupert I, the famous castle of the fifteenth century, the River Neckar and its adjoining orchards and vineyards. And he indulged in the numerous flirtations which were expected of the student, but hardly approved in a Jewish student: there were the Marias and the Emmas and the countless others. As a matter of fact Maria Zimmerman was a breathtaking beauty and a real baker's daughter and served as model and inspiration of the poem: *Et Mi Ohab* (Whom Do I Love). And Emma, the seamstress, was metamorphosed into 'Lenchen', the heroine of the poem by that name which recounts in embarrassing detail the rendezvous of the poet with the 'blond angel'. How the other girls affected Tschernichowsky's poetry must remain shrouded in the mystery of his artistic creativity.

It was also in Heidelberg that he met his future companion in life—Melania Karlovna von Gozias Gorbatshevitsh. A descendant of a noble Russian family—her relatives occupied high positions both in the Russian government and in the Russian army—and a spirited young lady, she experienced the rigours of prison life for her anarchistic involvements during the regime of Czar Nicholas II. Later, she was also to be jailed in the initial stages of Bolshevism. This independent-minded woman vaunted ultra-orthodoxy in revolutionary Russia and attended church services; religion, in her estimation, was the strengthening leaven of her mother country which was being debilitated and defiled by godless practices.

When the first and only daughter was born to them, they called her Isolda after the heroine of the Polish novel *Homo Sapiens* by Stanislaw Przybyszewski: Polish blood in the mother's family and romantic associations accounted for the name. The union of the poet and the young Russian aristocrat, unblessed by church or synagogue, was sealed for life. And Tschernichowsky was always proud of his highborn wife and her noble ancestry. The daughter married a Jew and settled in Haifa. Their child was brought up in the Jewish faith.[21]

The years in Heidelberg were undoubtedly the happiest years of the poet's life—in spite of his straitened circumstances. Though the honoraria for his poetry and the little money he received from his parents scarcely sufficed for the rental of a small room and the barest necessities of life, the poet's high spirits brushed aside such mundane inconveniences. Not only were some of his best love-lyrics written in Heidelberg, but some of his best idylls, the poems 'Deianira' and *le-Nokaḥ Pesel Apollo* (Before a Statue of Apollo) with their classic overtones, the powerful monologue with the ghastly echoes of the first Crusade 'Baruch of Mayence',[22] and the anti-prophetic *Me-Ḥezyonot Nebi' ha-Sheker* (From the Visions of a False Prophet). Some of these poems appeared in the second volume of *Visions and Melodies*, and some in the first big collection of his poems in 1911, in the editions of his poetry published by *Moriyyah* in 1914, 1918, 1921, 1923, in the ten-volume edition 1929–34, in the one-volume edition of his poetry published by Schocken in 1937, 1943 and 1953, and in the two-volume collection published by Dvir in 1966.

In 1903 Tschernichowsky moved to Lausanne where he spent three years of his life. It was easier for a Russian citizen to become a physician in Switzerland than in Germany. He showed a special predilection for surgery. But he also studied children's diseases and specialized in them in later years as a practising physician in Russia and in Palestine.

Life in beautiful Lausanne was difficult; the meagre literary earnings of the poet and the meagre subventions from his wife's relatives barely sufficed for their daily needs. Two narrow and uncomfortable rooms for a family of three were not conducive to creative work. The constant need for money, the petty loans and humiliations were sources of frequent depression. The years in Lausanne were, in fact, the most

21. A touching photograph of poet and grandchild faces page 32 of Joseph Lichtenbaum's book, *Sha'-ul Tschernichowsky—Toledotaw we-Yeẓirotaw*, Jerusalem, 1946.

22. See note 22 to Chapter 4.

unproductive in his literary career and he hardly wrote anything there. When the well-known and well-to-do Zionist,
Isaac Naiditsch, invited him to tutor his children in Interlaken,
he eagerly accepted and remained there for a few months.
From this enchanted spot he answered the query of his mentor
and friend, Joseph Klausner, why he did not react to the great
events of the day: the pogrom of Kishenev in 1903, the problem of Uganda which almost destroyed the Zionist movement, the death of Herzl, the Russian Revolution of 1905.
'You wish to know what I write and why I don't write . . . it
might be better, perhaps . . . if I explain why I write.

I write because I live, because I feel, at a certain hour, the
poetry of life. . . . The enigma of life is poetry, the most sublime
poetry there is and can be. And not merely poetry, but poetry
of victory, victory of matter over chaos, victory of being over
non-being, victory of life over death. . . .

Everyone of us . . . is a poem or—if he feels the poem—a
poet. . . . But the mire of the world, the stress and strain of
poverty make us forget the poetry and drown the soul in a
sea . . . of evil. . . .

The world consists of victors and vanquished. . . . And the
vanquished are more numerous than the victors. . . . I am the
bearer of the song of conquest and as a victor I want to make
my way in the world. Now as a Jew it is my destiny to be a
poet of defeat. . . . Yet even as a Jew I am the bearer of the song
of conquest. But, since the days of Kishenev, the Jew within
me feels the humiliation; while I, that sum total called I, am
still the bearer of the song of conquest. . . . '[23]

The letter was not a direct answer to Klausner's query—
except in the single allusion to an event of the day, to the
pogrom of Kishenev. But, in spite of the vague terminology,
it sheds light on the young and even on the later Tschernichowsky. He felt a new dawning within. The beaten son of a
beaten people made his way to a victorious affirmation of
life. This affirmation was a brew of many ingredients: the

23. The letter *in toto* appears in   pp. 154–5; in paraphrase *idem*,
Klausner's *Yoẓerim u-Bonim* II,   *Sha'ul Tschernichowsky*, p. 109.

Nietzschean will to power and the superman's arrogance, the trans-valuation of spiritual values à la Berdyczewski, the renewed interest in classicism. But, above all, it was a healthy diet which Tschernichowsky concocted, consciously and unconsciously, and assimilated into the very fibre of his being with vigour and originality.

It was in Switzerland that he wrote the poems *Ben Harim* (In The Mountains), '*Al ha-Mayim* (On the Waters) and the tragic idyll *Ke-Ḥom ha-Yom* (In the Heat of the Day) of which Mendele said: 'In Tschernichowsky's Garden of Eden God moves about "at the breezy time of day." '[24] In *Ben Harim* his attitude to Jewry is as critical as Bialik's and perhaps not uninfluenced by him. The people is 'a mound of corpses' in Tschernichowsky's eyes, 'withered grass' in the neo-Isaianic lines of Bialik. The great query of the generation—whither?—rouses the poet's impatience: to wherever voices call to ascend the heights, to wherever there is more brightness in the light of day; but the main thing is: not to stop, not to stagnate. Even these sentiments are half-personal, half-national. The poet is seldom the judge of his people.

Tutoring was an intermezzo between graduation and the actual practice of medicine. For more than a year—from August, 1906 to October, 1907—Tschernichowsky served as a physician in the city hospital of Melitopol and in the hospital of the *Zemstvo*—the semi-autonomous county administration. It was there that, for some unknown reason, he was imprisoned by the Czarist police and spent six weeks in jail. It may have been carefree talk which was not uncritical of the regime or contact with socialist youth which aroused the suspicions of the authorities. It was only thanks to the intervention of the local rabbi that he was released.

The harrowing experience resulted in an idyll *Ha-Kaf ha-Sheburah* (The Broken Spoon) which was written partly in prison and partly after liberation. Another idyll *Wa-Yehi 'Ereb wa-Yehi Boḳer* (And It Was Evening And It Was Morn-

---

24. *Ibid.*, p. III; Mendele's phrase alludes, of course, to Genesis 18:1.

ing), composed in 1937—thirty years after his imprisonment—also reflected the prison experience. And so did the two lyrical poems *Ra'am we-Ra'am Li Mebasserim* (Thunder Upon Thunder They Announce To Me) and, perhaps, *Shir Mizmor le-Tubal Cain* (A Song for Tubal Cain). In this quartet of uneven achievement the best of the poems is undoubtedly 'The Broken Spoon'. The fine description of a summer day which never penetrates the gloom of the prison; the talk of the prisoners and the humorous and illicit mending of a broken spoon; the philosophic discourse on the origin of prisons—all contribute to the rich and poetic texture of the idyll. 'And It Was Evening And It Was Morning' is a denunciation of capital punishment in a tone of righteous and rhetorical indignation. And the two lyrical poems are paeans of liberty.

For the next three years, from 1907 to 1910, Tschernichowsky was the official physician of the *Zemstvo* in the village of Yastrebenoe not far from Kharkov. But he also served many other villages which enriched his knowledge of the rural life of Jews and Russian peasants. It was from the fount of his rich experiences that he drew such idylls as *Berele Holeh* (Sick Berele) and the excellent small talk of simple Jewish women. And some of his best lyrical poems *Laylah ... Laylah ... Lel Kokabim* (Night ... Night ... Starry Night) and *Perahim le-Ahar Kazir* (Flowers After Harvest)—were written in Yastrebenoe. Sadness of mood is matched by sweetness of expression in both of them. No lyrical anthology of Hebrew poetry can afford to neglect them.

It was also during that period—in 1909—that he composed his lyrical masterpiece *'Olat Regel* (She—Pilgrim): the simple girl from the mountains of Galilee makes her way—together with a sacrificial kid and a basket of flowers—to the Holy City. Her monologue which is an inadvertent analysis of her feelings as she wends her bittersweet way to Jerusalem reads like a page from the Bible. The poem is a beautiful counterpart of Bialik's *Hozeh Lek Berah* (Seer, Go, Flee). One projects the image of a simple soul, the other—the image of a shepherd—seer; both extol uncorrupt simplicity. There is a feeling that such people as the Galilean girl found their perfect spokesman—disheartened and disillusioned but unbroken at the end—in Amos, the shepherd—seer.

The historical imagination of Tschernichowsky produced other poems on ancient themes in the first decade of the century: *Le-Ashtoret Shir u-le-Bel* (Song for Astarte and Bel) with its praise of instinctual joy, and *Mot ha-Tammuz* (Death of Tammuz) with its elegiac overtones on the seasonal departure of the god of fertility. The fact that a Hebrew poet dared to wrestle with the theme of paganism approvingly showed not only a deterioration of traditional values but a receptivity to new values among Jewish intellectuals in the early years of the century. Berdyczewski's advocacy of despiritualization found its poetic counterpart in Tschernichowsky's songs of pagan strength.

In 1910 the poet lost his official position. He stayed in the village of his birth for a while and, then, in the little village of Pishki near Grodno. In Mikhailovka he was moved to write his humorous idyll *Ma'aseh be-Mordecai we-Yukim* (A Story About Mordecai and Yukim)—a light-hearted account of a Jew and a Gentile who get drunk on *Simḥat Torah* and dream weird and hilarious dreams—not unconnected with the Jewish holiday. In Pishki he wrote 'The Charms of the Forest' and dedicated the poem to Mendele who celebrated his seventy-fifth birthday in 1910. Since his foreign diploma prevented him from the free practice of medicine in Russia, he decided to prepare himself for examinations at a Russian University. He successfully passed the final examinations for a certificate of matriculation—a condition for acceptance at a Russian University—and his doctoral examination at the University of Kiev. And for the next four years, from 1910 to 1914, he practised medicine in St. Petersburg (present-day Leningrad), without leaving the city except for a brief sojourn in Finland. There he began translating the famous epic *Kalevala* which appeared in Berlin in 1930 as volume four of his ten-volumed edition.

Life in St. Petersburg was hard, earnings were poor. Tschernichowsky rightly surmised that Jews would have no confidence in a physician who was a poet. So he practised in anonymity among Russians, meanwhile supplementing his medical livelihood with literary honoraria and literary and medical articles for the *Evreyskaya Encyclopedia*—the Jewish Encyclopedia in the Russian language. It is, perhaps, significant that his medical articles—poorly researched and superficially written—included 'Nervous and Mental Diseases Among Jews' as well as 'The Pathology of Jews'. This allegedly normal, healthy poet was sensitive to the abnormal and the unbalanced—in medicine and in poetry. Among the literary articles which he wrote for the Jewish Encyclopedia in the Russian language, the one on Russo-Jewish literature can still be read with profit. But his harsh, negative evaluation of that literature was not wholly justified. On the popular poet Simon Samuel Frug (1860–1916) he had previously written a favourable evaluation for the Encyclopedia.

In spite of tempting offers in Heidelberg, in St. Petersburg and in Berlin, Tschernichowsky refused to write poetry in Russian or translate poetry into Russian. Even Gorki who had heard of 'Elka's Wedding' was unable to persuade the poet to translate it for an *émigré* journal in Berlin. Tschernichowsky did, however, translate the idyll into Russian prose at the insistent request of the Russian poet Vladislav Feliksovich Hodasevich who converted it into poetry and published it in a Russian *émigré* journal.

At the beginning of the First World War, in September 1914, Tschernichowsky was drafted into the Russian army. He became military physician in a hospital in Minsk which had been established by the orthodox church. For his medical work in the hospital and at the front he was decorated by the government. The hospital authorities awarded him a Hebrew Bible.

In the years 1917–19 he served as vice-president of the Sanitary and Statistical branch of the Russian Red Cross. And in those years he also translated a textbook on anatomy which was designed to serve the needs of a non-existent Hebrew University. For the Eleventh Zionist Congress, held in Vienna in 1913, had decided to proceed with the establishment of a university in the Holy Land. Towards the end of the war the plan was revived, and a scientific organization was founded to prepare texts in medicine and in the natural sciences.

Towards the end of the First World War Tschernichowsky was invited by Abraham Joseph Stybel, the princely Maecenas of Hebrew literature for three decades, to translate the *Iliad* and the *Odyssey* from the original Greek. David Frischmann, the Hebrew poet and critic who became first editor of the quarterly *Ha-Tekufah*, intended to publish the first book of the *Iliad* in Tschernichowsky's translation in the first issue of the quarterly. When the proofs were sent to the poet, the latter forbade publication in a telegram. Frischmann, who had no Greek, had edited the translation in accordance with the German translation of Johann Heinrich Voss. Frischmann published the translation—together with an indelicate note—under his own name.[25] A literary scandal of minor proportions was brewing for a time. Tschernichowsky was not deterred. He went on with his translations of the Greek epics and completed them in the early twenties.[26]

25. See *Ha-Tekufah* I, 1918, p. 298. Tschernichowsky never forgave Frischmann for mishandling and mistreating the translation of the *Iliad*. Twenty-two years after the publication of the first book of the *Iliad*, he referred to the event in very intemperate language. See unpublished letter of May 7, 1940 from Tschernichowsky to Klausner in the Manuscript Collection of the National and University Library of Jerusalem.

26. At the end of the typescript of the *Iliad* which is among the treasures of the National and University Library of Jerusalem the poet notes the cities where he translated the masterpiece and the dates of translation: Petrograd, Bardiansk, Odessa, Berlin, 1917–1923. He seems to have forgotten Istanbul. But he alluded to his translation of the *Iliad* in that city in one of his stories. See Saul Tschernichowsky, *Sheloshim u-Sheloshah Sippurim*, Tel-Aviv-Jerusalem, 1941, p. 106. Klausner is not correct in stating that Tschernichowsky finished the translation of the *Iliad* in Istanbul. See his *Sha'ul Tschernichowsky*, p. 179. The entire *Iliad* appeared in volumes VIII and IX of the ten-volumed edition of Tschernichowsky's works, Tel-Aviv, 1932; 1933; again, together with the *Odyssey*, in a larger volume published by Schocken Publishing House, Jerusalem and Tel-Aviv, 1954.

During the war years he also wrote *Mi-Manginot ha-Zeman* (Out of Contemporary Melodies) with its overt allusions to the tragic consequences of slaughter for the individual Jew and the Jewish people. Another poem of those tormented years, *Manginah Li* (I have a Melody), is a sort of poetical credo: the poet traces his spiritual ancestry to pre-Canaanite times, to the generation of the wilderness that conquered a land for landless people. This poem, written in 1916, was playfully called by Tschernichowsky the 'Balfour Declaration before the Balfour Declaration'.

Twice in his life Tschernichowsky felt the urge to enunciate a credo, a confession of faith: when he was nineteen, he wrote his popular though immature *Ani Ma'amin* (I Believe). The poem, set to music, was later sung by all students of Hebrew. It achieved, indeed, a greater popularity than many more deserving poems by Tschernichowsky. The boyish confessional is a disarming plea to a girl not to laugh at his belief in man, in liberty, in social justice, in friendship, in national co-existence, in the resuscitation of Jewry. In the final stanza, Tschernichowsky expresses the hope that in the era of fulfilment of his ideals a new type of poet, alert to the beautiful and the sublime, will arise in the world. And this young poet will be crowned with flowers from Tschernichowsky's grave.

This confessional of an idealist at the turn of the century is an adumbration of the other confessional, written twenty-two years later: 'I Have a Melody'. The poet has found himself at last. He no longer indulges in generalities but vaunts his specific aspirations, his conceptions of liberty, his brand of personality. The road from 'I Believe' to 'I Have a Melody' is the road from immaturity to maturity, from adolescent expression to manful art.

The Russian Revolution exerted a devastating impact on Russian Jewry. The slow attrition and final strangulation of Hebrew literature were only incidental by-products of a policy which made war on religion and opposed Zionism, which eliminated most forms of Jewish education and discouraged all attempts to follow a Jewish pattern of life.

Tschernichowsky suffered in the initial years of the Russian Revolution. Hunger stalked the country, chaos reigned in many parts of Russia. Whites battled against Reds in savage combat. Most military hospitals were closed after the conclusion of the war with Germany and the Central Powers. Fear of starvation forced the poet to abandon the capital and seek his luck in more familiar places: at first in the Crimea and then in Odessa where he spent several years—from 1919 to 1922. The conditions in that city, however, were as apalling as everywhere else. The purchase of a loaf of bread necessitated many hours of waiting in long queues; water had to be drawn in buckets from wells; nights were long and dark; the cold—even in southern Russia—made the winter intolerable.

The city of Odessa passed from hand to hand—from the control of the Ukrainian Skoropadski and Petlura to the Reds and from the Reds to the Whites. Tschernichowsky served many ephemeral governments for inadequate compensation. His private practice was far from lucrative. A hearty meal was a rarity in those days which he described with pathos and humour in the poem *Mayim she-Lanu* (Water Kept Overnight)[27] and in the story *Ba-Laylah* (At night).[28] To add to the tribulations: a severe form of pneumonia almost felled his strong body.

In those difficult post-war days, in the year 1920, Tschernichowsky's translations of Anacreon appeared in Warsaw under the imprimatur of the Stybel Publishing Company. The Greek poet of wine, women and song appealed to the Hebrew poet: as a young man he had published an Anacreontic poem in the very first collection of his poems. At the same time he brought out his translation of Plato's *Symposium*. But his *Phaedrus* was not published because a Hebrew translation by Zevi Diesendruck, the well-known scholar, had already appeared. In those

27. On the *double entendre* of the words *Mayim she-Lanu* in the Hebrew title of the poem see The Babylonian Talmud, *Pesaḥim* 42 a.

28. The story appeared in Tschernichowsky's Collected Works VII, Tel-Aviv, 1932, pp. 63–9.

unfortunate years Tschernichowsky wrote most of his sonnets, the ballad *Pa'amonim* (Bells) and the idyll 'Elka's Wedding'. *Shir ha-Ahabah Asher le-Sha'ul* (Saul's Love Song), the last poem that Tschernichowsky wrote in Odessa, was a narcissistic whimsy on a central theme in his work.

In 1922 Tschernichowsky left Russia, and spent four months in Istanbul working on the translation of the *Iliad*. In the same year he settled in Berlin where he lived till 1931. There he translated Longfellow's *Evangeline* from the original, the semitic epic *Gilgamesh* from a German translation, the *Odyssey* which was revised in Palestine, Molière's *Le Malade Imaginaire*, Goethe's *Reineke Fuchs*, Shakespeare's *Twelfth Night* and *Macbeth*.[29] In Berlin he also published numerous feuilletons and stories, a volume of children's poems *he-Ḥalil* (The Flute) and a book of *Shirim Ḥadashim* (New Poems) which were written for the most part in Odessa. But he did not practise medicine in Berlin where he would have had—according to German law—to treat foreign patients only, and he was not accepted as a physician in Palestine, though he solicited a position. His fame as a poet was apparently detrimental to his practice: no one had confidence in a physician who served the muses. In medieval times Jews had a long tradition of famous physician-poets. But that tradition died in the twentieth century: fragmentation and parcelization of knowledge had become the norm and the fashion. The *uomo universale*, even if he were by some miracle to re-emerge, would be distrusted and derided.

Fortunately for the poet, a wealthy admirer and a friend since student days, Shalom Alexander Riwkin, invited him to spend a considerable part of 1924–5 in his villa in Swinemünde. There he finished his fragmentary translation of *Kalevala* which he had begun in 1911, there he wrote several ballads and love poems, and completed the only play he ever wrote:

29. No complete translation of *Macbeth* by Tschernichowsky is available. Fragments were published in Palestinian periodicals but not in any collected editions of the poet's work. See Klausner's *Sha'ul Tschernichowsky*, p. 182.

Bar Kohba.[30] Though it had been solicited by Nahum Zemah, the founder of the Hebrew National Theatre, *Habimah*, it was never produced except in amateur performances. It is an interesting commentary on the poet and on the theatre that *Oedipus Rex* was also not produced in his translation.[31] But *Twelfth Night*, perhaps the weakest attempt at translation by Tschernichowsky, was produced by *Habimah*.

Poverty was a constant threat in the post-war years. At times the poet suffered hunger and was unable to satisfy his elementary needs. Though inflation ruined the Stybel Publishing Company, Stybel helped the poet from time to time and paid him handsomely for his translation of *Gilgamesh*. Bialik who was also the director of a publishing company—*Dvir*—was either unwilling or unable to aid him. But Tschernichowsky's bitterness did not lessen his admiration for the great contemporary poet.

A meagre source of income supported the poet in the twenties. The new publishing firm *Eshkol* undertook to publish books in Hebrew and the *Encyclopaedia Judaica* in German and in Hebrew. Tschernichowsky was invited by the editor, Dr. Jacob Klatzkin, to edit the section on natural sciences and medicine for the two Hebrew volumes of the *Encyclopaedia* which appeared in 1929 and 1932 respectively. He also wrote his only literary monograph for *Eshkol*: *Immanuel of Rome*. Though there is an undoubted kinship between Tschernichowsky and the Jewish poet who lived 600 years before him, the evaluation lacks critical penetration and thorough research. Not a single page of the monograph is devoted to Immanuel the exegete

30. Tschernichowsky had serious doubts about the play. He was anxious to read it to Klausner and to hear his opinion. See unpublished letter of February 13, 1925 from Tschernichowsky in Swinemünde to Klausner in Palestine in the Manuscript Collection of the National and University Library of Jerusalem.

31. In an undated letter to Klausner from Berlin Tschernichowsky complains that *Habimah* is playing *Le Malade Imaginaire* in his translation without permission. The letter is in the Manuscript Collection of the National and University Library of Jerusalem.

and Immanuel the philosopher.[32] Yet his commentaries on the Bible—most of them in manuscript, very few in print—yield rich information on the encyclopaedic range of his mind. And his scientific, moral, and mystical interpretations of Holy Writ should have delighted Tschernichowsky whose intellect roamed over wide areas of knowledge.

Like so many scholars since Steinschneider, he did not appreciate Immanuel's wit. The self-deprecatory remarks of the Italian poet—the seeming unoriginality of his contributions to exegesis—are more than offset by the allusions to his vast erudition. For he says of himself:

> ... you gave no sleep to your eyes nor slumber to your
> eyelids till you gathered all the pearls of wisdom,
> and set them in a commentary on God's perfect Torah. ...
> You have not neglected grammar, literal meanings, original
> explanations, hidden mysteries and wonderful riddles. ... [33]

The entire monograph by Tschernichowsky briefly recapitulates the few biographical facts known about the poet and endeavours to analyze the *Maḥbarot* (Compositions). But the analysis can be reduced to casual remarks which do not shed fresh light on an important figure in the history of Hebrew poetry. Tschernichowsky's study is, at best, an eclectic amalgam of well-known opinions on Immanuel—the light-hearted, charming, humorous, brilliant sonneteer and story-teller in verse, poet of irresponsible love and precursor of the renaissance among the Jews of Italy.

In 1924 Tschernichowsky was invited to visit Budapest. Among the participants in one of the splendid banquets in his honour were the president of the Hungarian Academy of Sciences and Hungary's minister of education who addressed him in a speech as 'King of Hebrew poets'.

32. For the first study in depth of Immanuel's contribution to exegesis and philosophy, see F. M. Tocci's publication and analysis of Immanuel's commentary to the first chapter of Genesis: *Il Commento di Emanuele Romano al Capito I della Genesi*, Rome, 1963.

33. See *Maḥberot Immanuel* XXVIII, lines 640–642 in Dov Yarden's edition II, Jerusalem, 1957, p. 538.

The fiftieth anniversary of the poet in 1925, which was not as sumptuously celebrated as the jubilee of Bialik two years before, had one important result: a ten volume edition of his writings was urged and projected by Nahum Sokolov who was influential in Zionist circles and by Dr. Benzion Katz who was responsible for obtaining financial aid. It was published in the years 1929–34, and the proceeds furnished the poet with a livelihood for some time. But he was so poor that he often went coatless even during the cold winters in Berlin. No wonder that he considered moving to Madagascar and even to the Soviet Union where he hoped to practise medicine. Both countries were then offering inducements to combat epidemics and contagious diseases. Requests for a position in Poland and in Palestine which he visited for the first time in 1925 were refused. Later, the oldest High School in the latter country appointed him physician to its pupils. But the salary was so small that he had to return to Berlin after a while. Part of *Shirim Le-Ilil* (Poems for Ilil) and *Le-'Olim be-Hare Yehudah* (For the Pioneers on the Mountains of Judah) were written in Tel-Aviv during his brief sojourn.

A grant of 700 dollars from the Matz Foundation in New York eased the desperate situation, while a visit to Lithuania and Latvia afforded him much pleasure. Thousands of students were enthusiastic in their reception of the poet, and to them he dedicated his poem *Ha-Pesel* (The Statue).

When the quarterly *Ha-Tekufah* was revived in Berlin in 1928, Tschernichowsky became one of its three editors. Though remuneration was slight, the work was arduous. Tschernichowsky encouraged young writers of talent, but he was inhospitable to poor writing even if it was submitted by authors of renown. Only three volumes of *Ha-Tekufah* (24, 25, 26–7) appeared in Berlin between the years 1928–30. Tschernichowsky invested unsparing efforts in his editorial job amid comparative freedom from want. His co-editors—Dr. Benzion Katz and Dr. Simon Rawidowicz—were well-suited to edit the non-belletristic sections of the quarterly.

In November of the year 1928 Tschernichowsky arrived in

America where he spent five months. His was a double task: to find subscribers for the books and the quarterly of the Stybel Publishing Company and to solicit financial aid for the vast network of Hebrew educational institutions under the aegis of the Tarbut foundation in Lithuania. He was not over-successful in the first task and only moderately successful in the second—with the aid of Dr. Zemah Feldstein, one of the administrators of Tarbut.

The enthusiastic welcome, the banquets in his honour, the articles in the press, the readings and lectures in various cities on Hebrew metre, on Greek and Hebrew poetry, on medical terminology to Hebrew speaking physicians in New York—all had an exhilarating effect on the poet. New York and Boston, Cleveland and Chicago welcomed him with open arms. Philadelphia even collected a sum of money to cover the publication costs of his stories—the sixth volume of his collected writings. A more than passing infatuation with a young woman in the United States—a psychological flashback to Heidelberg—resulted in a series of love poems.

At the end of the twenties the poet moved to Fichtengrund, an hour's journey by train from Berlin. There he spent the final years of his exile in Germany, 1929–31. In dire poverty but in rustic surroundings he wrote some of his best lyrics.

In 1931 Tschernichowsky settled in Palestine where he remained—with three brief interruptions—till his death in 1943. The interruptions occurred in 1935, in 1936 and in 1939. In 1935 he was the guest of the Finnish government which celebrated the hundredth anniversary of the publication of *Kalevala*[34] by Lönnrot.[35] Tschernichowsky was decorated with

34. Kalevala is the name of a legendary district in Finland. It is based on the personal name Kaleva, also a legendary figure. Originally a man of good repute, he came to be identified with demon or devil. Since most of the actions of the folk poems, collected by Lönnrot, took place in Kaleva's district, they were called by him *Kalevala*. See *The Kalevala—A Prose translation with Foreword and Appendices* by Francis Peabody Magoun, Jr., Cambridge, Mass., 1963, pp. XIII–XIV; 368–70.

35. Elias Lönnrot published an edition of *Kalevala* in 1835: it con-

the Order of the White Lily. In 1936 he was in Buenos Aires as a delegate of the Hebrew Pen Club. In 1939 he found himself in Warsaw—on the way to a Pen Club Congress in Norway, but returned in haste because of the outbreak of the Second World War.

Klausner, the loyal friend, found some means of support for the poet in Palestine. At his behest, the poet was to edit the material for a medical dictionary which had been left unfinished by Dr. Aaron Meir Masie—physician, scholar, Hebraist. Although Tschernichowsky had only two aides, he finished his labours in two years and proof-read the bulky tome for another two years. For the editorial revisions he received 25 Palestine pounds per month during the first two years and 12½ pounds for the next two years. Out of this royal sum he sent more than half his income to his wife who stayed with their daughter in Paris where she studied bacteriology.

A stiff upper lip to mere acquaintances, a tale of woe to intimate friends: this is how Tschernichowsky played the pathetic game of life in Palestine. To Dr. Alexander Isaiah Spiegel he writes on October 1, 1934:

> You also wish to learn about people's attitude towards me. I think you will readily understand. The attitude towards me—towards a man without 'pull'—is as it should be in a land where everything depends on 'pull'.
>
> As to my practice: some people don't know that I am a doctor; and those who know that I am a medical man imagine that I am getting rich on Hebrew literature; while those that ply the literary trade think that I am getting rich on medicine. If I were a German refugee, something would be done for me, of course, some positions would be created, all sorts of sinecures. . . .

The fortieth anniversary of his literary work was celebrated

---

tained thirty-two poems and 12,078 lines; an enlarged edition in 1849 contained fifty poems and 22,795 lines. There is also a *Proto-Kalevala* of 1834 which remained in manu-script for nearly a hundred years. It was brought out by the Finnish Literature Society in 1929. *Ibid.*, pp. 363; 365; 379.

with a public banquet. It was on that occasion that Bialik gave generous praise to Tschernichowsky. And Tschernichowsky, on the occasion of Bialik's sixtieth birthday, published an encomiastic appraisal of his great contemporary. An important by-product of Tschernichowsky's anniversary was the publication of seven out of the ten-volume edition of his works: it enabled him to live without worry for a while. The poet participated fully in the life of Palestine under the Mandate. He supported labour, and protested against the judgment in the Arlozorov case; he did not condone the policy of restraint —*Havlagah*—in 1936 when Arabs attacked villages and burned crops, and he voiced his sentiments in such poems as *Ba-Mishmar* (On Watch) and *Parashat Dinah* (The Case of Dinah). When the Peel Commission proposed a partition of Palestine which was eagerly accepted by the Zionist Congress in Zürich, Tschernichowsky voiced his protest against partition in *Sabta Kak Hayetah Omeret* (Grandmother Would Say) and in *Medinah Yehudit* (Jewish State).

The sixtieth birthday of the poet was celebrated in 1935 wherever Hebrew was read and spoken. Many articles appeared in his honour, and some of his poems were translated into several languages. The city of Tel-Aviv granted him honorary citizenship. In 1936 his wife and daughter moved to Jerusalem where his daughter married shortly afterwards. The birth of a grandchild was a source of joy. At that time Schocken had contracted to become his publisher for eight years and pay him a monthly salary of thirty pounds. Although he had to reduce his work as a school physician, he had an assured livelihood for the first time in his life. And that happened almost at the end of his life. But, since the poet had previously obligated himself to *Dvir*, he had to pay an indemnity of three hundred pounds to that publishing house. Five pounds were subtracted from his monthly salary for five years. In response to the autobiographical questionnaire sent to Tschernichowsky by *Genazim*—the literary archives of Israel—he mentioned the sum of thirty-five Palestine pounds as his average monthly income. And that was all: no stocks, no bonds, no real estate, no financial assets of any kind. The questionnaire was signed on December 5, 1941—less than two years before his death.

In 1937 the Schocken Publishing Company published a one volume edition of his works, and in 1940 a new volume of poems written between 1936 and 1939, entitled *Re'i Adamah* (See, O Earth) which was awarded the Bialik Prize in 1941.

This robust poet had suffered from *angina pectoris* for some time. In the summer of 1941 symptoms of leukemia complicated the state of his health. Yet he continued his literary and quasi-public labours. In September of 1941 he made a radio address in Russian beamed to Jews in Russia: it emphasized the unity of the Jewish people. The concluding sentence became an oft-quoted slogan: 'Hear, oh Israel . . . the people of Israel is one.'

In the same year he published his book of thirty-three stories and, in 1942, his tales for children: *What was and what was not*. He even thought of rewriting a novel which he had almost completed in Leningrad during the First World War and which he could not smuggle out of Russia. He also saw his translation of the *Odyssey* in print in 1942. The publication, aided by Dr. Magnes, the first president of the Hebrew University, was financed by the Goldberg Fund and Schocken.

On the fiftieth anniversary of the publication of his first poem a special issue of the literary monthly, *Moznayim*, was devoted to his work. The City of Tel-Aviv established the Tschernichowsky Prize for translations from classics and natural sciences in his honour and made him the first recipient of the prize for his translation of the *Odyssey*.

In 1943 the Schocken Publishing Company again published his poems in one volume which contained his poetry till 1939. His last poems appeared after his death—in 1944—under the title *Kokebe Shamayim Rehokim* (Stars of Distant Heavens). A poem under that title was his last act of creation—about a month before his death.

On the thirteenth of October 1943, the first night of Succoth, he fell ill. He joked with his physician, Dr. I. L. Rokeah: 'One has to die, younger people than I die nowadays.' Then he

added: 'But here, in a home that belongs to a monastery ... '
He did not finish the sentence. He died in peace—on property
belonging to the Russian Orthodox Church.

He was buried in Tel-Aviv. Thousands escorted the bier,
and his son-in-law recited the *Ḳaddish*. There were no eulogies:
Jewish law frowns on them during festivals. Besides, the will of
the poet, executed January 17 and 18, 1942 and signed by him
July 2, 1942, states explicitly and tersely in the opening words:
'No eulogies, no flowers.'

Chapter 2

NEW POETIC VISTAS

A. *Proto-Judaism*

LIKE all modern literatures Hebrew literature has felt the corroding impact of technology on religion. A specious scientism, profane in challenge and impact, has overlaid and overwhelmed all sacral attitudes to life. Poetry which, in the happy phrase of Goethe, anticipates knowledge, has been aware of religious laxity for more than one hundred years. The publication of Baudelaire's *Les Fleurs du Mal* in 1857—an important milestone in world literature—was a manifesto of despair and cynicism and ennui attendant on the dissolution of religious values. The substitution of art for religion—art for art's sake as it was advocated by Mallarmé—was not the extreme end of that road. For art, including literature, degenerated into *dada* which is the preference of non-sense to sense. Expressionism and surrealism also tended to break the moulds of sense. They were the impasses of art and literature. Even the extremism of a genius like James Joyce has not flowered in a new school or a new movement. It was merely a magnificent memorial at the dead-end of literature.

But the great literary figures of this century were not only symptoms of religious decay. They were also living symbols of religious regeneration. Chief among them in Anglo-Saxon countries was an American who emigrated to England, T. S. Eliot, and an Englishman who settled in America, W. H. Auden. In Hebrew literature, a whole galaxy of poetic stars—Bialik and Tschernichowsky, Shneour and Greenberg—transformed an arid agnosticism into religious energy. Because of them the Jewish past is still the inexhaustible fountain of faith.

Even before the end of the nineteenth century the rise of

Jewish nationalism displayed all the characteristics of a secularized religion. The last of the 'enlightened', Judah Leb Gordon, called for a Nietzschean transvaluation of values before Nietzsche. In poem after poem he castigated the excessive spirituality of Judaism: the prophets were leaders who led to the destruction of the First Commonwealth, the sages were guilty of the destruction of the Second Commonwealth. The true guides like king Zedekiah (597–587) who rebelled against Babylon and Simon Bar Giora, one of the commanders in the revolt against Rome in 66 C.E. were constantly harassed by an almost treacherous group of spiritualizing leaders. This was the burden of Gordon's poetic message. It influenced the Nietzschean thinker Micah Joseph Berdyczewski as well as the poets Jacob Cohen and Zalman Shneour. And it achieved its profoundest expression in Tschernichowsky. His vaunted paganism and his flirtation with Hellenism were the negative aspects of that expression. They emphasized such elements in foreign cultures as licentiousness, exuberance of physical strength and warlike aggressiveness. In other words: what Judaism abhorred was shown to be desirable, and what Judaism regarded as weakness was extolled as a source of strength.

But, with the sure instinct of the poet, Tschernichowsky realized that a search for the real essence of Judaism is even more important than the poetic annihilation of Judaism. Taking his cue from Berdyczewski, he seems to have found his Judaism in the misty ages which preceded the conquest of Canaan. This proto-Judaism he idolized and idealized. His was a song that derived from ancient days, his was 'the blood of the blood of the conquerors of Canaan',[1] who had transmitted to their children's children the vision of a country stretching from the Euphrates to *Arabia Deserta*. The God of Israel was not the bloodless abstraction of the medieval sages; in his terrestrial rather than celestial majesty he preferred

1. See the poem *Manginah Li* which was written in Minsk in 1916. Schocken's one-volume edition of Tschernichowsky's collected poetry, Jerusalem and Tel-Aviv, 1953, p. 278.

the earth and its peoples to the empty spaces of heaven.[2]

That was the positive Judaism of Tschernichowsky which adumbrated the future course of Hebrew poetry and fathered an excessive nationalism. The hysteria of a Jacob Cohen, of an Uri Zevi Greenberg, of an Isaac Lamdan, have all drawn their inspiration from Tschernichowsky. He was the *fons et origo*, the source and origin of their poetry.

Even the bizarre beliefs and opinions of the 'Canaanites'[3] who achieved a short-lived notoriety in the fifties of this century are rooted in the poetry of Tschernichowsky. For they hold that the entire post-exilic history of the Jews since the fall of Bar Kohba in 135 C.E. is a harmful episode, a shameful memory, an irrelevant intrusion into the present. Thus the Talmud which guided all aspects of Jewish life to the very threshold of modern times, medieval philosphy and the subsequent Hebrew literature which was created outside Israel must be consigned to everlasting limbo. Even Zionism—the most creative self-expression of Jewry in the last seventy years—has not met with the approval of the 'Canaanites'. For them only Hebrews, born in Israel and bred by a native culture, constitute a nation. Jews are merely a community.

Though Tschernichowsky might have been horrified by this extremism, he cannot be absolved from a certain recklessness in his poetry which fostered the strange brood of 'Canaanites'. He himself did not discard later Judaism, but he anthologized it only for its elements of heroism in his long poem 'Baruch of Mayence' and in a series of shorter poems which praised the fearlessness of the pioneers in their reconquered

2. See Tschernichowsky's poem *Me-Ḥezyonot Nebi' ha-Sheḳer* which was written during the student days of Heidelberg. Schocken edition, p. 101.

3. The literary aberration, known as Canaanism, with its deep repercussions in the political and social life of the young state of Israel and with its antecedents in the nineteenth century, deserves a full-length monograph. A sensitive evaluation of the movement can be found in Baruch Kurzweil's article *Mahutah u-Meḳorotehah Shel Tenu'at ha-'Ibrim ha-Ẓe'irim*, *Luaḥ ha-Areẓ*, Tel-Aviv, 1952, pp. 107–29.

land. His real love, however, was reserved for the realm of proto-Judaism which meant—to him at least—the realm of the Semitic myth.

Now myth is characterized as 'purely fictitious narrative usually involving supernatural persons'. This lexical definition does not go far enough. With the boldness of profundity and innocence myths attempt to penetrate the impenetrable. They are poetic discourses on the eternal themes of human and non-human existence. If the creative powers of Tschernichowsky were roused by myths, it was because the texture of his personality—a mixture of depth and innocence—corresponded in some way to that of an ancient myth-maker. Myths of Babylonians, Egyptians, Jews and Greeks as well as myths of Finns and Slavs flowed into his poetry in such profusion that they outweighed all other elements. Tschernichowsky may be justly called the only myth-making poet in the history of Hebrew literature.[4] With characteristic boldness and self-awareness he uses the term 'the mythology of our family' at the very outset of his autobiography.

But is not a myth-making poet in Hebrew a paradox foisted upon the Jews by an ironic fate? Is not pagan mythology the antithesis of the rigorously ethical monotheism that has served as the ideal guide of the Jews for more than three millennia? A myth is, after all, a story associated with polytheistic rites. It may be aetiological in essence, assigning a fictitious cause to a real or imagined event. It may be theogonic, explaining the origin of gods. It may even, as nature myth, theologize phenomena of nature. Yet, always, it binds the human and the superhuman with a multideic chain.

Jews, like all ancient peoples, exulted in their myths in the dim beginnings of nationhood. The stories of creation, Cain and Abel, the sons of God who married the daughters of men, the deluge, were the common mythological stock of the restless tribes that roamed the Fertile Crescent. Lilith, the ever-popular demoness in ancient times and often re-incarnated as

4. For substantiation see Eisig   of Myths' in *Commentary* I, 1946,
Silberschlag, 'Tschernichowsky: Poet   pp. 48–50.

the monstrous woman in literature, in art, in cinema, is recorded as a night-monster in a solitary instance in the Bible—Isaiah 34:13-14—in company with wild-dogs and ostriches, wild-cats and jackals and satyrs.[5]

In post-biblical literature she is an ubiquitous figure. And Hieronymus identified her with the Greek Lamia—a queen deserted by Zeus and robbed of her children by Hera. Rahab, the sea monster who unsuccessfully defied God, is paralleled by Poseidon, god of the sea, who defied his brother Zeus.

The Bible is full of vestigial myths. A sizeable volume by the English poet Robert Graves and the Jewish anthropologist Raphael Patai endeavours to reconstruct the Hebrew myths in the Book of Genesis.[6] The texts of Ugarit,[7] dating back to 1400 B.C.E., have thrown a flood of light on the Canaanite pantheon which exhibits common features with the Hellenic gods. Even at that time Greeks and Jews seem to have shared an international civilization which was built on an eastern Mediterranean foundation. This community of interests and traditions does not detract from the purity of monotheism. It rather enhances the religious genius of the Jews who alone among ancient peoples transformed myth into monotheism.

The poet grasped intuitively what the scholars confirmed at a later date: that the pagan Greeks and the early Hebrews had wide areas of culture in common. He did not hesitate to identify himself with the worshippers of Tammuz-Adonis, Bel and especially the Semitic Venus, Astarte. He was even moved to compose a cycle of liturgical sonnets to the sun, which in their perfection of form and their pagan homage to the forces of nature have no equal in Hebrew literature. The austere lines

5. See also Isaiah 13:21.

6. See Robert Graves and Raphael Patai, *Hebrew Myths*, Garden City, New York, 1964.

7. Hundreds of clay tablets and clay fragments from the fourteenth century B.C.E. were excavated by C. F. A. Schaeffer at Ugarit (Ras Shamra in Northern Syria) between 1929 and 1939. They have preserved fragmentary liturgies and rituals as well as portions of mythological epics in cuneiform alphabet and in a Canaanite dialect with remarkable affinities to Phoenician and Hebrew.

seem carved by a master sculptor who, overwhelmed by the beauty and warmth of light, translates his religious awe into religious art.

Yet these sonnets to the sun were inspired by a prophetic text (Ezekiel 8:16) and a Mishnaic tradition (Sukkah 5:4). Perhaps Tschernichowsky overworked his romantic attachment to the remote past. He did so with the enthusiasm of a lover who has found his world in the object of his affection and discovered, almost inadvertently, a forgotten source of poetry and emotion.

From Semitic mythology it was only a step to the early mythological world of other peoples. His vast work of translation, which includes the Babylonian epic *Gilgamesh*, the Greek epics, the Finnish epic *Kalevala* and parts of the Icelandic *Edda*, is neither an accident nor the result of economic exigency: it was a basic necessity of his poetic personality.

B. *Fusion of Judaism and Hellenism*

TSCHERNICHOWSKY is the first poet in the long history of Hebrew literature who may claim credit for a *rapprochement* between classical and Hebrew poetry. What the Jewish philosophers of the middle ages accomplished within the limits of philosophy, he achieved within the confines of poetry. Instead of borrowing, as they did, ideas and arguments from Plato and Aristotle, he appropriated devices which were pertinent to his art, namely, figures of speech and metric variety. Thus he widened the scope of Hebrew literature and, at the same time, inaugurated a tradition of far-reaching consequence.

It may seem strange that it did not occur to any poet before him to utilize the rich resources of Hellenic literature. Perhaps the fear of mythology, tinged as it was with idolatry, accounted for the lack of interest in Hellenic *belles-lettres* and a consequent impoverishment of Hebrew poetry. When Moses Hayyim Luzzatto introduced Eros with bow and arrow into his first play *Ma'aseh Shimshon* (The Story of Samson), he converted the Greek deity into a Hebrew abstraction *Ḥesheḳ* (Desire) and divested it of its grace and mischief. Even such modest excursions into the realm of mythology rarely occurred in Hebrew poetry which repeated, with monotonous insistence, the twin theme of *Galut* and *Ge'ulah*, exile and redemption, to the exclusion of most, if not all, others.

Ignorance of Greek, on the other hand, should not have deterred the poets any more than it prevented the philosophers from absorbing Greek influences. Just as for the latter 'the translations of Aristotle both in Arabic and in Hebrew have preserved to a remarkable degree not only the clear-cut analyses of the text of Aristotle's works but also the exact meaning of his terminology',[8] the numerous translations of the classics in European languages could have attracted the Hebrew poets and exercised a fruitful influence upon their work. John Keats, for example, cannot be fully understood without reference to Greek literature in spite of the fact that he knew no Greek.

Hebrew poetry which, unlike Hebrew philosophy, had strong ties with the synagogue eschewed, then, the idolatrous literature of the Greeks. Judah Halevi who did not hesitate to profit from Greek philosophy in his *Kuzari* sounded the classical warning in his poetry: 'Let not the wisdom of the Greeks beguile you; it bears no fruit but only flowers.'[9] When, toward the end of the nineteenth century, Nietzschean ideas were given wide circulation in Hebrew literature through the propagandist zeal of Berdyczewski, the way was paved for a new interest in Greek literature. As a classical scholar Nietzsche relied on Greek philosophy and Greek literature to sanction his revolutionary transvaluation of values. And an interest in Nietzsche led to a concomitant interest in Hellenic literature. It was not, however, a clash of Greek thought and Jewish faith as in Hellenistic Egypt, nor an attempt to balance Platonism or

8. See H. A. Wolfson, *Crescas' Critique of Aristotle*, Cambridge, 1929, p. 7.

9. Halevi, *Divan*, ed. H. Brody, II, p. 166; cf. also Halevi, *Kobez Shiraw*, ed. A. E. Harkavi, p. 19 and the interesting note by S. D. Luzzatto; for a discussion of the passage, cf. L. Strauss, 'The Law of Reason in the Kuzari', *Proceedings of the American Academy of Jewish Research* XIII, 1943, p. 62.

Aristotelianism or both with Judaism in a neat system of philosophy as in Spain, nor even a headstrong preference for Abrahamism as against Atticism as in the writings of Samuel David Luzzatto, but a friendly absorption of a rich literary heritage into a renascent literature.

With Tschernichowsky, however, it was more than a friendly absorption. It was a case of literary osmosis. An early acquaintance with Homer, a formidable love-affair in his youth and, last but not least, a good classical education, facilitated the process. In an early poem *Sirṭuṭim* (Outlines)—a parallel to the Byronic hymn 'The Isles of Greece'[10] in the third canto of *Don Juan*—Tschernichowsky evoked a vision of Hellas, 'the cradle of beautiful and mighty souls', the land where 'bloomed the songs of Homer, the plays of Sophocles'.[11] The sympathetic attitude toward Greece gave an unusual buoyancy to the poem which introduced the elegiac distich into Hebrew poetry and, incidentally, widened its metric range. The novel metre which was first used by Callinus of Ephesus in the seventh century B.C.E. achieved great popularity in Greece and persisted in Byzantine literature beyond the age of Justinian, but it rarely appeared in European literatures. Goethe, with an unfailing instinct for the *mètre juste*, used it in his *Römische Elegien*. It was also the best choice for a poem like 'Outlines' which teemed with romantic longings for a lost culture. For the dactylic hexameter, followed by the elegiac pentameter, imparted a stately nobility of rhythm to the verses.

Two other poems on Greek themes emphasize Tschernichowsky's love for Greece: 'Deianira' and 'Before a Statue of Apollo'. In 'Deianira' the well-known myth is used by the poet as a short appendage to a long panegyric on the olive-groves and pine-forests of the Greeks, on the marble temples which are likened to the frozen dreams of a poet, on the beautiful goddesses and the strong gods. And in 'Before a Statue of

10. Translated by Tschernichowsky in *Hadoar*, June 20, 1941. See also the Schocken edition of Tschernichowsky's poems, pp. 690–5.

11. See the Schocken edition of Tschernichowsky's poems, pp. 105–106.

Apollo' which was probably responsible for the ill-fated epithet
'Greek' which was tagged onto his name, he endeavoured to
find a link between the Jewish God of the desert and the Greek
god of light. It would be erroneous to conclude that Tschernichowsky preached frank idolatry or, in contradistinction to
Samuel David Luzzatto, asserted the superiority of Greek to
Hebrew culture. The poet merely felt that the Jews were sufficiently removed from the pagan world to borrow safely some
of its saner qualities. He was captivated by a dissimilar and disparate literature, and endeavoured to illumine the dismal dom-
ain of Hebrew poetry with an equivalent of the Provençal *gay
saber* which Nietzsche popularized in *Die fröhliche Wissenschaft.*

Significantly, the poet used in 'Deianira' the oldest metre in
Greek poetry: the dactylic hexameter. But even this common
poetical device seemed like an innovation. When Sabbato Vita
Marini (1690?–1748) attempted to translate Ovid's *Metamorphoses*
which were composed in dactylic hexameters, he used Giovanni
Andrea dell' Anguillara's Italian version and, consequently,
abandoned the original metre for the *ottava rima*.[12] Similarly,
Micah Joseph Lebensohn translated from Schiller's German
translation part of the second book of Virgil's *Aeneid* into Hebrew in a different metre,[13] and Marcus Rothberg who translated Goethe's hexametric *Hermann und Dorothea*, changed the
metre—*metrisch frei übersetzt*—as he honestly informed the
reader on the title-page—and the name of the poem.[14] It re-

---

12. For a modern and metrically
correct Hebrew translation of
parts of Ovid's *Metamorphoses* by J.
Friedman, cf. *Ha-Teḵufah* III, 1918,
pp. 449–79; XII, 1921, pp. 103–18;
XXVI–XXVII, 1930, pp. 420–6.

13. The title *Harisot Troyah* is an
imitation of Schiller's *Die Zerstörung
von Troja*. In his preface to the translation Lebensohn assumes errone-
ously that he has translated the third
and the fourth book of the Aeneid.

Cf. M. J. Lebensohn, *Shirim*, Berlin
1924 p. 143. For a plausible explana-
tion of the error cf. J. Fichmann,
Ha-Baʿayot be-Shirat Mikal, *Ha-
ʿOlam*, August 6, 1942.

14. *Newe ha-Ẓedeḵ* (*Wohnung de
Tugend*) *oder Hermann und Dorothea*
Warsaw, 1857. An excellent translation in the original metre was made
by S. Ben-Zion who took cogniz-
ance of his predecessor's work. Cf
S. Ben-Zion, second edition o

mained for Tschernichowsky to use the hexameter in such profusion that it also became one of the common metres in modern Hebrew poetry. The idylls which established his reputation and his chief claim to immortality were written, almost exclusively, in dactylic hexameters. This literary *genre*, with its long line of antecedents in Hebrew literature from the biblical *Ruth* to Judah Leb Gordon's *David and Barzilai*, had no definitive metric mould. In Greek literature Theocritus, the father of the Hellenic idyll, used the Homeric hexameter for his charming descriptions of simple people. It was an act of poetic justice that Tschernichowsky translated one of his idylls, 'The Syracusans', into Hebrew.[15] Unfortunately, he adhered to the dactyl with far greater rigidity than either Homer or Theocritus who often changed it into a spondee in the first five feet. The result was a slight rhythmic monotony both in his idylls and in his translations of the *Iliad* and the *Odyssey*. His best and longest idyll, 'Elka's Wedding' seems to have caught the spirit of the Greek epics. Externally, it resembles neither the *Iliad* nor the *Odyssey*. Instead of their twenty-four books it boasts of six cantos (*Shirim*). Nevertheless, the noble rhythm of the dactylic hexameter, the rich body of folk-lore incorporated in the idyll, the simplicity of characterization, the Greek vocables from the Hellenistic period—all seem to have been inspired by reading and translating Homer. And chronologically, the gestation and composition of the idyll coincide with the translation of Homer.

In one of his last poems 'I've Nothing of My Own' Tschernichowsky expresses the sincere desire that, since he is destined to be poor and destitute, a private pantheon adorn his bare room: statues of Moses, Isaiah, Astarte, Shakespeare, Goethe,

---

Hermann we-Dorothea, Berlin, 1923, p. 115, footnote. A third and recent translation of the German work by Joseph Lichtenbaum, the Hebrew poet, was published in Tel-Aviv in 1967.

15. The translation which appeared in *Ha-Tekufah* XXII, Warsaw, 1924, under the title *Ha-Sirakusot O Hogegot Hag Adonis* was not reprinted in any edition of the collected works of Tschernichowsky.

Plato and Homer, 'that great seer of a world of beauty'.[16] Thus
Tschernichowsky again paid tribute—as he had done in the
youthful 'Outlines'—to the genius of Greece which reached its
perfect expression in the epics of Homer and the dialogues of
Plato.

Among the hellenizing poems by Tschernichowsky 'The
Statue' holds a unique place. Though the theme is Greek, the
sentiment is Hebrew. In measured, unrhymed lines—as befits
a classical subject—the poem evokes the dedication of a statue
of Zeus in the presence of its sculptor and emissaries from the
entire Greek world. The awe of the people suddenly confronted
by the statue, the ecstatic genuflections and the roars 'kalos,
kalos, kalos' (beautiful, beautiful, beautiful) so reminiscent of
the Hebrew Ķadosh, Ķadosh, Ķadosh (holy, holy, holy) are
described with proper unrestraint as the occasion warrants. But
the attitude of the sculptor is Hebrew rather than Greek. For he
alone stands upright amid the prostrate crowd, unmoved by
the statue which he has fashioned but awed by the deity, more
beautiful than the statue, 'more pure, more divine'.[17] It was
God who hovered before his eyes in visionary splendour while
he worked and it was God who remained, even after his act of
creation, an unreached, unreachable ideal. God as an abstraction is Hebrew rather than Greek in concept.

Even in his stories Tschernichowsky wrestled with the problem of Hellenism. He never really resolved the conflict and the
confrontation with the alien culture. King Agrippa I (41–4)
speaks with the poet's accents when in the story *Be-Karme
Agrippas* (In Agrippa's Vineyards), he confesses to the Chief
Justice of the highest court in the land:

> ... We, the Hellenizing Jews, are the best Greeks there are,
> disciples of Plato and Socrates. ... Greek philosophers were
> my teachers, Roman centurions my guides, and precisely be-
> cause they wished to make me a citizen of Athens or a Roman

16. See the Schocken edition of   17. *Ibid.*, p. 462.
Tschernichowsky's poems, pp. 590–
593.

knight, I became a Jew. I am with the Jew in his sorrow, I feel his pain, I cherish his festivals, I am offended when he is hurt.[18]

Jew and Greek: that ever-present dichotomy overwhelmed Tschernichowsky. He drew upon the resources of Greek philosophy and withdrew into his Hebrew shell. He drew upon the resources of Greek poetry and enriched his own with its boundless variety. Homer was a constant presence. In the story *Be-Palatin Shel Herodion* (In the Palace of Herodium)[19] the disillusioned and disappointed Berenice quotes verses from Homer (*Iliad*, xiv, 321–5) in the original Greek. It was partly due to the influence of Homer that Tschernichowsky shifted his attention from the lyric to the epic and effected a literary revolution.

For it is generally conceded that the genius of Hebrew poetry is predominantly lyrical. The utterances of the prophets, the hymnal raptures of the psalms and, in medieval times, the poems of Gabirol and Halevi, are mostly curt translations of ethical passion into verse. And since the very word 'lyrical' is associated with a musical instrument, lyrical verse tends to rely on musical devices: alliteration, repetition, rhyme and assonance. These devices are not missing from Tschernichowsky's poetry which is predominantly epic,[20] but they are not as prominent as in the work of his contemporaries. The idylls are the best products of his muse. And their chief asset—like the chief asset of any epic poem—is plasticity and not musicality. Although Tschernichowsky was not endowed with the descriptive powers of Homer, he created clear images rather than a melody of feelings.

While the name of Bialik is associated with memorable lines or stanzas, the name of Tschernichowsky is inseparably linked with such characters as Baruch of Mayence, Gitele, Velvele,

18. See *Israel Argosy* 6, ed. I. Halevy-Levin, Jerusalem, 1959, pp. 41–2. The translator is Sulamith Schwartz.

19. *Mo'znayim* XVI, 1943, pp. 76–81.

20. It is false, however, to assert, as some critics do, that Tschernichowsky's work is devoid of lyrical elements. Cf. *Ha-Shiloah* XXXV, 1918, p. 124.

Elka and a host of others that people his poems and idylls. These characters are drawn simply and carefully, with a view to their statuesque effect rather than their psychological subtlety. Delineation of character was the secret of Homer and Theocritus. It was also the secret of Tschernichowsky who, like his ancient prototypes, employed direct rather than indirect speech on a very large scale. Unlike so many modern poets who were fascinated by 'what's difficult'[21] and who delighted in the cult of the obscure and the abstruse, he was the most perspicacious of poets. His language may be difficult at times, but his image, his design and his purpose in most poems are crystal clear.

Epic poetry is chiefly an art of narration which dodges and overcomes the constant danger of prosaic intrusions. It is a difficult art, requiring skill and a special imagination. Homer, the acknowledged master of epic poetry, had an indisputable share in the vivid poetical narratives of Tschernichowsky. Both poets dwell on the daily routines of life with an effortless love. They show craftsmen at work and they describe people at table out of sheer joy in physical existence. The episodes embellish the narrative and frequently heighten an emotional effect or a dramatic suspense. Yet both poets—Homer in his epics, Tschernichowsky in such idylls as 'Circumcision' and 'Elka's Wedding'—have achieved that ineffable harmony in composition which Aristotle called 'the unity of incidents'.[22]

Another of Tschernichowsky's qualities was strengthened, perhaps, by his contact with the Greeks. The general tenor of his poetry, even where it is sad or funereal, scintillates with a vaunted exuberance of spirits. Towards the end of the nineteenth century it was fashionable to popularize Greek civilization as a fount of perpetual gaiety.[23] Tschernichowsky was a

21. The phrase is taken from the poem by William Butler Yeats which begins with the line: 'The fascination of what's difficult. . . . '

22. *Poetics* 1450a 15: the Greek phrase is ἡ τῶν πραγμάτων σύστασις.

23. Cf. J. Klausner, *Yozerim u-Bonim*, III, pp. 189–90; for a discussion of the problem, cf. M. Croiset, *Histoire de la Littérature Grecque*, 4th ed., Paris, 1928, I, pp. 17–19.

victim of this fallacy. But while an erroneous assumption may be fatal to a philosopher or scientist, it has often proved to be a boon to the poet. In fact, the best poets flourished at times when sets of stable ideas, true or false, were shared by poet and public alike.

Tschernichowsky who accepted the assumption that Hellenism signifies joy and affirmation of life became the conscious singer of spring, strength and love. With his departure from the lyric and his translation of Homer, cherished by his countrymen as myth-maker, educator and pre-eminent poet,[24] he ushered in a new era in the development of Hebrew literature. The great Hebrew epic, so clumsily cultivated by such second-raters as Wessely and Shalom Cohen, at last had a chance to become a reality.

Meanwhile classical Greek literature has experienced another revival in Hebrew garb. Klausner, Kaminka, Diesendruck, Leon Roth, Span, Benzion Benshalom, Muntner and Dykman have translated important masterpieces of Greek literature, most of them directly or indirectly influenced by Tschernichowsky. Thus Greek literature which borrowed, translated and paraphrased from Semitic sources in its pre-Homeric phase completes its circular journey from the Semitic orbit into the Semitic orbit. The possibilities of this felicitous marriage of two classical literatures are as illimitable as they are fruitful in the role they are destined to play in the development of modern Hebrew literature.

Recent archeological discoveries have added considerably to

24. Homer made a theogony for the Greeks (Herodotus II, 53) and educated Hellas (Plato, *Republic* X, 606 E). Moreover, 'he has made poetry about practically everything' (Dio Prusaensis, *Oratio* XXXIII, 11). The vitality of Homer is also attested by Aeschylus who admitted that his plays were mere slices from the great banquets of Homer (Athenaeus, *Deipnosophists* VIII, 347 E). The judgment of the ancients is often corroborated by modern scholars: 'Von den zwei Seelen, die im Herzen des Altertums wohnen, ist er [Homer] die eine; die andere ist die platonische.' Cf. J. Geffcken, *Griechische Literaturgeschichte* I, Heidelberg, 1926, p. 11.

our knowledge of interrelations between the two countries. Surprising similarities have been discovered—beside the well-known approximations of the alphabets—in the mythologies,[25] in the music,[26] and in the architecture[27] of the Canaanites and the Greek peoples.[28] More remarkable than these are the resemblances in social institutions, especially in the almost identical attitude to the feminine ideal. Chryseis is praised for her beauty and her works. Sir William M. Ramsay noted that in Phrygian dirges a woman or a wife is often extolled for her beauty and her household works which, on gravestones, are represented by 'a distaff and spindle and cooking-pot'.[29] But he failed to consider the obvious biblical analogy, the praise of the 'woman of valour' which, significantly, ends with the word 'her works' (*Ma'asehah*).[30] As for literary similarities, it is now generally accepted that the origin of pre-Homeric songs such as the death of Linos, for instance, was Semitic.[31] Gilbert Murray who likes to emphasize the superiority of the Greek epics to the biblical stories cannot help noting the similarity in the growth of the Bible, especially the Pentateuch, and the Homeric epics.[32]

25. See W. F. Albright, *Archeology and the Religion of Israel*, Baltimore, 1942, p. 91; for an Ugaritic source of the myth of Hercules and the Hydra, cf. C. H. Gordon, *The Loves and Wars of Baal and Anat*, Princeton, 1943, p. XII.

26. Albright, *op. cit.*, p. 82; pp. 125–6.

27. *Ibid.*, p. 143; pp. 214–15, n. 44.

28. In an article on 'The Achaeans' William K. Prentice offers a cautious and interesting suggestion: 'It seems to me at least possible that the real Achaeans were originally a non-Greek people. . . . Perhaps they came from the East.' Cf. *American Journal of Archeology* XXXIII, 1929, p. 208.

29. W. M. Ramsay, *Asianic Ele-*ments in Greek Civilization*, New Haven, 1928, p. 103, n. 2; p. 114.

30. Proverbs 31:31.

31. Cf. R. C. Jebb, *Homer: An Introduction to the Iliad and the Odyssey*, 7th ed., Glasgow, 1905, pp. 1–2; similarly V. Bérard, *Les Phéniciens et L'Odyssée* II, Paris, 1903, p. 11; for oriental influences on Greek legends and tales, cf. J. Geffcken, *op. cit.*, I, p. 11.

32. Cf. G. Murray, *The Rise of the Greek Epic*, 4th ed., Oxford, 1934, pp. 107–19; 169–72; 193–4; R. W. Livingstone, on the other hand, notes that 'in our Bible . . . we find the elemental feelings of Homer and an expression even more direct'. Cf. *The Legacy of Greece*, ed. R. W.

Homeric scholars have often availed themselves of the biblical narratives for purposes of literary comparisons. They are too obvious and too significant to be neglected.

Whether Tschernichowsky was fully conscious of the striking similarities between Jews and Greeks in the numerous domains of life and letters or not is less important than the aid that they must have given him in the work of translation. As a poet he probably felt such similarities more than he knew them. It was because of his empathy that he succeeded in imparting a biblical rather than post-biblical flavour to his Hebrew versions of the *Iliad* and the *Odyssey*. With the sure touch of a master he took advantage of such common peculiarities of style in Homer and the Bible as the introductory formulas of the speakers and such turns of speech as parechesis and antithesis.

The translation of the Greek epics marks a milestone in the development of Hebrew literature. For, next to the Bible, the *Iliad* and the *Odyssey* have been the most potent influences in world literature. And together they form a trio of almost indisputable literary excellence and eminence, stemming as they do from a hoary antiquity when poetry was an inseparable component of song[33] and appealed to the emotions primarily. With that ancient magic which primitive poetry possessed in a larger degree than modern poetry, they have quickened our perceptions and enlarged the range of our spiritual life.

Livingstone, Oxford, 1921, p. 257; T. R. Glover steers a middle course: 'Homer and the Bible are different books, fundamentally different, in outlook, aim and construction. Yet of each the same thing can be said— the book built a race.' Cf. *The Challenge of the Greek*, Cambridge, 1942, p. 216.

33. This is true of the older poetic portions of the Bible such as Exodus 15:1–18. It is interesting to note that for Homer the poet is a singer, ἀοιδός—an equivalent of the Hebrew מְשׁוֹרֵר and not ποιητής. The latter word was unknown to him.

Chapter 3

NARCISSISM

THE ATTITUDE of Saul Tschernichowsky toward King Saul
is a very complex and complicated affair. It is love with narcissistic overtones; it is angry contempt for the mighty and famous
adversary, David; it is a battle against indiscriminate injustice,
as epitomized by David. Sometimes, all three factors inter-
twine and interplay in Tschernichowsky's poems on Saul.

As a boy of twelve Tschernichowsky wrote a poem on
'Uriah the Hittite', condemning David and praising Uriah.[1]
As a man of sixty he castigated King David in his poem 'Perek
be-Anatomiyyah' (Chapter in Anatomy), maintaining that this
progenitor of the Messiah was an expert in the art of overt and
covert killing.[2] Strangely, post-biblical literature reflected compassion towards Saul and resentment against David: 'Saul
sinned once; it brought calamity upon him. David sinned
twice; it did not bring any calamity upon him.'[3]

In the same Talmudic passage Saul's uprightness is praised
'[Saul was] like a one-year-old infant who had not tasted sin.'
In his autobiographical sketch Tschernichowsky made a significant confession: 'I don't know why, but for a long time I
nursed a grudge against all who were renowned as saints, and
I was always on the side of king Saul. Perhaps the name had
something to do with it.'[4] His own name and the name of the
revered grandfather Saul Karp—these were the narcissistic
factors which made Tschernichowsky sensitive to the name
Saul. Contempt for the powerful and defence of the powerless

---

1. See Tschernichowsky's autobiographical sketch in *Ha-Shiloah*
XXXV, August, 1918, p. 103.

2. Only once, in the thirteenth
sonnet of the cycle 'On the Blood',
Tschernichowsky mentions the 'son

of Jesse' with approval. But then it
is not the king but the poet who is
praised as one of the liberators of
mankind.

3. *Yoma* 22b.

4. See note 1.

reflect the great currents of social endeavour at the turn of the century. They bred the revolution of 1905 in Russia and they resulted in the Bolshevist uprising of 1917.

Modern Hebrew literature like much of rabbinic literature seems to be on the side of Saul.[5] Judah Leb Gordon favoured Saul against Samuel in his 'Zedekiah in Prison', and Micah Joseph Berdyczewski praised Saul for his nobility, his heroism, his tragic fate, and condemned David for his treacheries and tricks against friends and foes, for his unabashed opportunism and evil-mindedness. These writers—Gordon and Berdyczewski— were the two literary revolutionaries who clamoured for a new, and largely unfavourable attitude to prophecy in general and extreme spirituality in particular. Tschernichowsky inherited the revolutionary thread and spun a web of dazzling beauty in his five poems on Saul. He wrote them during various periods in his life. The first one, the ballad 'Endor' (1893), captured the penultimate tragic episode in Saul's life—the planned encounter with the witch of Endor.[6] Although the poem follows the biblical narrative faithfully, it manages to recreate a frightful moment—perhaps the most frightful—in the turbulent career of Saul. In swift amphibrachic couplets the poem moves to its foreseen finale: the 'awesome despair' and the suicide. But the poet stops short at the 'awesome despair'—the last two words in the poem—and recreates in the tense darkness, punctuated by fitful flames and the smoke of the witches' cauldron, a quick reminiscence of Saul's happy youth. This is a fine example of Tschernichowsky's contrapuntal gift: in the midst of tragedy his protagonists remember idyllic moments of life. Thus, the hero of the celebrated poem 'Baruch of Mayence' reminisces about the idyllic life with his wife and two daughters amidst the fire which he has set to the town. Saul's reminiscences of his youth are Tschernichowsky's most valuable elaborations of the biblical account.

In the dialogue with Samuel, Tschernichowsky also manages

5. On Saul in talmudic and world literature see Solomon Eidelberg, *Parashat Sha'ul ha-Melek be-Shirato* *shel Sha'ul Tschernichowsky*, *Hadoar*, August 9, 1963, pp. 656-7.

6. 1 Samuel 28:7-25.

to induce a new tone. In the biblical narrative Saul is tired and desperate. In one single sentence he also conveys his helplessness: 'I am very distressed for the Philistines make war against me . . . I have called you to let me know what I should do.'[7] In the poem Saul appears as the accuser with a legitimate complaint. He had been the contented shepherd who was asked to sacrifice his happiness on the altar of service; he had been the unwilling victim of unsolicited greatness.

Tschernichowsky's 'Endor' is not a confrontation of king and prophet—as Gordon's 'Zedekiah in Prison'. It is the confrontation of a man in distress and a divinely inspired but disappointingly ineffectual prophet. There is perhaps a shrinkage of theme in Tschernichowsky's poem. The theological and teleological problem is reduced to a human, all-too-human equation. But the loss of grandeur is compensated by a gain in intensity on the plane where, ultimately, it matters most—on the individual plane, on the level of confrontation of the self with the self in a mirror, be it the mirror of a prophet or the mirror which mocks all our endeavours.

In the poem 'Al Ḥorbot Bet Shan (On the Ruins of Bethshan), the ghost of Saul wanders near the walls of the city where the Philistines fastened his body after cutting off his head. He seeks revenge and he is ready to command an obedient army at the time when the dead shall arise; but he knows that God will prevent him. He, therefore, commands revenge with ḥesed (=love or kindness). This is an enigmatic line. It was interpreted by a recent critic as an ironic statement.[8] But irony is not Tschernichowsky's forte. 'What it says' is always different in kind or degree from 'what it means'.[9] And Tschernichowsky is a master of the direct rather than the indirect statement, the canny insight rather than the uncanny clairvoyance. There is the likelihood, then, that the young Tschernichowsky followed the biblical account: ' . . . but my ḥesed shall

7. *Ibid.*, 28:15.

8. Jacob Bahat, *Sha'ul ha-Melek be-Yezirato Shel Sha'ul Tschernichowsky, Ha-Ḥinnuk* XXXVI, 1963, p. 11.

9. Northrop Frye, *Anatomy of Criticism*, Princeton, New Jersey, 1957, p. 81.

not depart from him [David's progeny], as I took it from Saul'.[10]

The poem *Ha-Melek* (The King) attempts to illumine another facet of Saul's personality: the *vis mystica* of kingship. In an encounter with a band of prophets in Ramah, the king is greeted as 'the annointed of God, greater than his brethren'. And he is told that, although he lacks sanctity, he will suffer from the touch of wings that hurry through eternities 'to fathom the secret of absolute freedom'. In an ecstatic dance with the prophets the king merges with the band of prophets and drops, one by one, all insignia of superiority—the crown, the harp, the sword, the royal robes. Only then, in stark nakedness, does he achieve sameness with the band: group unity and the prophetic gift. The poet whose name was Saul achieved identification with king Saul. He divested him of all royal prerogatives as if to say: the true king is one of the people and one like the people. A talent for humility is the secret of superiority.

The poem *'Al Hare Gilboa* (On the Mountains of Gilboa) was written in 1929 in Fichtengrund. It depicts a mood of courage in the face of adversity, faith in the face of calamity. In the swiftly moving dialogue between Saul and his armour-bearer who tries to protect him in vain, between the king and the heralds who announce to him in breathless succession that his sons Jonathan, Malchishua and Abinadab are dead in battle, the royal zeal is reborn. Let the trumpets sound and resound, let the earth tremble, let the ranks of the stumbling and falling be filled. These are heroical pyrotechnics rather than heroism, nationalist slogans rather than a *cri de coeur*. 'On the Mountains of Gilboa' is perhaps the weakest of Tschernichowsky's poems on Saul. It is too swift a reaction to events which were shaking Jewry at the time—the slaughter of innocents by Arabs in mandatory Palestine.[11]

10. 2 Samuel 17:15; 1 Chronicles 17:13.

11. Yet Kurzweil argues that in the poem 'On the Mountains of Gilboa' Tschernichowsky reached 'the pinnacle of ballad artistry'. See Baruch Kurzweil, *Bialik we-Tschernichowsky*, Jerusalem–Tel-Aviv, 1960, p. 221.

The poem *Anshe Ḥayil Ḥebel* (A Band of Valiant Men) is a
ballad built on the last three verses in the first book of Samuel.[12]
They tell about the tragic finale of Saul: how 'valiant men'
took the body of the king and his sons from the wall of Bethshan and buried them under the tamarisk tree in Jabesh.
According to another version which is also utilized in the poem
the bones of Saul and his sons were buried under the terebinth
in Jabesh.[13]

Tschernichowsky depicts the stealthy and solemn march of
the valiant men who carry 'upon a pole between two' the
bodies of the king and his sons through mountainous terrain
at night. The allusion to the well-known phrase in the Bible[14]
heightens the sorrow. The spies sent by Moses brought back
indications of a land of plenty, 'a branch with one cluster of
grapes, and they bore it upon a pole between two'. The valiant
men carry a burden of death. When they bury Saul—under
the terebinth or the tamarisk—they leave no sign, no monument to his greatness. Neither the Philistines must know the
location of the grave nor the upstart king who is contemptu-
ously called 'the slave of Bethlehem'. It is best that someone
remember in song the generous heart of Saul who fell like a
lion on his sword.

'A Band of Valiant Men' is a tone poem; it is one of the
finest, most musical dirges in modern Hebrew literature. And
in a literature so rich in elegiac poetry, it is not easy to write an
epitaph of such intensity.

'Saul's Love Song', written in Odessa in 1922, has only a
tenuous connection with the biblical Saul. It is based on a biblical verse: 'And there ran a man of Benjamin. . . . '[15] The man
of Benjamin, according to Rashi, is Saul. Tschernichowsky
accepts the designation and depicts Saul in the ecstatic words
of his beloved. The poem begins with a dialogue between the
girl and her friends. Youthful exuberance is the dominant tone
of the girls who have frolicked and gambolled by the fountains
and by the towering aloes. In gay exhaustion they have come

12. 1 Samuel 31:11–13.   14. Numbers 13:23.
13. 1 Chronicles 10:12.   15. 1 Samuel 4:12.

to their friend to see her wardrobe and her jewels, her household gods and her love-goddess Astarte. Then the subject of the dialogue moves to a more personal plane, to the lover. His prowess, his fearlessness, his armour, and his prize possession—the camel with the golden-grey hair—are described with breathless, youthful abandon. Then comes the tragic moment. The beloved sees her lover's mother and sister by the fountain. The mother cries, the sister grieves, the beloved understands. The Philistines, the Edomites, the Dodanites, the kings of the East have invaded neighbouring territory. The lover went out to fight the enemy but has not returned. Night after night she watches from the balcony on the roof and she tortures her soul with the tragic possibilities in store for her lover—hard labour, slavery, death in battle. One morning he knocks at her door, wounded and exhausted. Nobly she urges him to go to his mother who has spent her days in an agony of uncertainty.

'Saul's Love Song' is written in the style and vocabulary of the Song of Songs. Oriental in flavour and in the detailed description of the charms of the lover rather than the beloved, it is also much more coy, much more restrained than the Song of Songs. But its greatest offense is its deliberate imitativeness. It reads like a bowdlerized version of the Song of Songs. Even Klausner, the uncritical admirer of Tschernichowsky, concedes that it is 'an imitation of the Song of Songs'.[16] Yet he adds characteristically if perversely: but it is 'a very original imitation'.

If Tschernichowsky strove for an apotheosis of Saul, he failed. His poetic gifts were equal to the evocation of simple girls like Elka or 'She-Pilgrim' who are miniature character-studies of unaffected purity. But the anonymous beloved of Saul and Saul himself are weak versions of biblical prototypes in the Song of Songs. The poet's best monument to king Saul remains the dirge on 'A Band of Valiant Men'.

16. J. Klausner, *Sha'ul Tschernichowsky*, p. 168.

Chapter 4

THROUGH FORM TO SIGNIFICANCE

A. *Sonnet*

TSCHERNICHOWSKY is the master of form in Hebrew poetry. No one before or after him has achieved a similar variety of *genres* and a similar wealth of metric innovations. Consciously and deliberately he experimented with new types of stanzas instead of the prevalent quatrains, with new poetic quantities instead of the ubiquitous trochees. For he suffered, as a young poet, from the poverty of technique in modern Hebrew poetry. In one of the few essays which emerged from his pen, in 'Bialik-Master of Form', he traced most forms in Bialik's poetry to the lowly Italian canzone.[1] But the title 'master of form' belongs rightfully to Tschernichowsky rather than Bialik.

He is the sonneteer *par excellence*. Now the sonnet has a venerable tradition in Hebrew literature. Giacomo da Lentino fathered the form in thirteenth-century Sicily, the Hebrew poet Immanuel of Rome (1270?–1330?) introduced it to Hebrew literature. For more than 600 years it was a favourite with Hebrew poets in Italy, with Immanuel Francis, Rachel Mor-

---

1. *Rimmon* III, 1923, p. 41. For an analysis of Bialik's metres cf. B. Z. Benshalom, *Mishkalaw Shel Bialik*, *Keneset* VII, 1942, pp. 28–52. After the monumental researches of Robert Lowth scholars of the school of David Heinrich Müller professed to discover, on a parallel basis to the Greek choruses, strophe, antistrophe and epode in Hebrew hymnology. This theory has been abandoned in favour of a less elaborate strophic structure for the majority of the psalms. For a critique of the various theories, cf. C. F. Kraft, *The Strophic Structure of Hebrew Poetry*, Chicago, 1938, pp. 21–31. It should be remembered, however, that the typography of the Hebrew Bible which resembled a prosaic rather than a poetical text, had incalculable results in impoverishing form and metre in modern Hebrew poetry.

purgo, Joseph Almanzi, the Luzzattos-Samuel David and Ephraim and Moses Hayyim. But Tschernichowsky was the most profuse and the most original sonneteer in Hebrew.

One of his earliest poems is a sonnet which regards nature not as a sweet locale of dreams but as a theatre of tensions. And it is nature which is chosen as an imitable entity: the despairing poet must feel ashamed at the sight of waves which, broken on the rocks, return time and again to battle against them. He must feel ashamed, too, at the sight of the rocks which although buffeted by the waves, proudly lift their hearts and heads on high (Not Moments of Repose).[2] In another youthful sonnet the sight of mountains evokes a plea. The poet asks God to summon the storm from his storm chambers and sweep an enslaved people to freedom (In the Mountains).[3]

In a later sonnet written after the pogroms which swept the Ukraine in the aftermath of the First World War, the poet chided his people in gentle terms. No gravestones mark the skeletal remains which are merely obstacles in the path of the ploughing ox; and the dead know not why they are furrowed by the ploughshare, why they have lived and why they died prematurely[4] (The Grave).

The sonnet cycle 'On the Blood'[5] is perhaps the most poignant expression of frustrated hopes and soaring aspirations. Only imagination is, according to the poet, the source of renewal, only the priests of beauty are the hope of mankind. Rivers of blood, shed by holy hangmen—reformers who beguile the people with songs of freedom and promises of justice —sometimes turn the desert into a 'a grassy dell'. But the finale of their tune is chain and scaffold. The great reformers are the great destroyers of mankind. Misled by abstractions they, in turn, mislead the people. As long as they have no power they coo and woo with modest mien. As soon as they achieve power they become destructive wolves. What Tschernichowsky did not perceive—and what Hobbes saw with an

2. The Schocken edition of Tschernichowsky's poems, p. 10.

3. *Ibid.*, p. 209.

4. *Ibid.*, pp. 323–4.

5. *Ibid.*, pp. 385–95.

unmatched lucidity—was the apparent harmony of unregenerate leadership with their unregenerate charges. The true leaders
of mankind—the poets—bridge the past and the future, spread
hope and save the world with song and music. This is a naïve
version of the exaggerated Shelleyan creed that 'poets are the
unacknowledged legislators of mankind'. This is a naïve religion of beauty, harmless in doctrine and ineffectual in practice.
Tschernichowsky translated 'The Cloud' as a young man and
admired Shelley throughout his life. And he unconsciously
echoed the creed of the English poet in the gory cycle of sonnets which were undoubtedly inspired by the cruelties of both
Whites and Reds at the end of the second decade of the
twentieth century.

Conceptually and theoretically the cycle of sonnets 'To the
Sun'[6] is an innovation in Hebrew poetry, for it is a liturgical
collection of verses in praise of the sun-deity. In execution it is
the most perfect exemplar of sonnets in the Hebrew language.
Such was the impact of their strangeness on publication that
Klausner furnished them with a running commentary in the
foremost Hebrew periodical of the day.[7] But the fact is that the
poems—in spite of stylistic difficulties—are self-explanatory.
They reiterate a favourite theme in depth: the poet's attitude
to ancestral religion and his sympathetic appreciation of paganism. But they also aspire to a new creed. Its novelty consists
in the centrality of the sun. The poet is conscious of paradox
and anachronism. The paradox stems from the fact that, as a
Jew, he worships what pagans worshipped: an element of
nature. The anachronism lies in the fact that such a personal
cult is an impossibility after centuries of scientific evolution.
Perhaps the poet believed that a new faith in a god of joy, a god
of sunlight, must be fashioned out of the disparate religions of
the world.

As a good Jew Tschernichowsky based his quest for a new
religion in Jewish tradition and prefaced the cycle of sonnets to
the sun with a Mishnaic text: 'Our fathers when they were in

6. *Ibid.*, pp. 291–301.   7. *Ha-Shiloaḥ* XXXIX, Jerusalem, 1921, pp. 451–61.

this place turned with their backs toward the Temple and their faces toward the east, *and they worshipped the sun toward the east*' (Sukkah 5:4). The end of the quotation—an echo of Ezekiel 8:16—was underlined by the poet who translated religious awe into religious art, warmth and light into a cosmic principle.

B. *Idyll*

THE IDYLLS are among the most characteristic products of Tschernichowsky's muse. The conservative form—the oldest metric device of the Greeks—matches the conservative content: traditional Jewry in a rural milieu. Yet form and content were new, almost revolutionary, in modern Hebrew poetry. The form of the Greek epic and the theme of rural Jewry were both daring innovations.

If the myth was Tschernichowsky's favourite theme, the idyll was his favourite form. It may be said without undue exaggeration that he was as much the father of the Hebrew idyll as Theocritus was the father of the Greek idyll. There is, indeed, a close relationship between these two poets, separated though they are by more than two millennia. Both modelled themselves on Homer. Both borrowed from him the hexametric dactyl for their idylls and both observed and depicted the details of everyday life as he did. But Homer dealt with gods and heroes. Theocritus and Tschernichowsky preferred simple folk and simple talk, the joys and sorrows of rural life, the influences of the seasons on man and nature.

The poetic reflection on the life of Jews in rural, southern Russia was Tschernichowsky's gift to Hebrew literature. Before him, Hebrew writers had confined themselves to the traditional urbanism of their people. When they wanted rural themes, they turned to history. Tschernichowsky was the first modern Hebrew poet to celebrate his native district. And he had the power to lift segments of life from regional obscurity to the status of literature. In his idylls Tschernichowsky achieved mature serenity. No overt fight against accepted norms, no iconoclastic stance mars the inner repose of his long hexa-metric lines. The Jew is at peace with nature; he is the good neighbour of the Gentile. Gitl in 'Boiled Dumplings', Eliakim in 'Circumcision', Velvele in 'In the Heat of the Day', Berele in 'Sick Berele', Mordecai and his only daughter Elka in 'Elka's Wedding', Eli in 'Eli', Simḥah in *Simḥah Law Dawka* (Not Exactly Simḥah)—all these are unsophisticated charac-ters who seem to have been born before the Fall. Young Berele and young Velvele are not like the boys of former generations, for study is not their only concern. On the cont-rary, exultation in physical strength is their vaunted glory. As if to underline the contrast with Bialik's portrayal of the ever-diligent student, Tschernichowsky uses, almost at the begin-ning of the idyll 'Eli', a half-line which is reminiscent of the opening of Bialik's *Ha-Matmid*: 'There are in the reaches of the diaspora. . . . '

But the reaches of the diaspora depicted by Tschernichowsky are full of strong men like Eli who are not only well-built, but almost heroic in daily feats of valour. As for religious observ-ances, men like Eli are apt to treat them perfunctorily. Even the older folk are not rigid in their observances, now that they have felt the impact of Zionism and the rise of socialism. Yet Tschernichowsky is able to describe traditional ceremonies and observances—all the abundant Jewish life in the villages of Southern Russia—with Homeric abandon, with the skill of an accomplished craftsman. The Russians—the coachman, the servant-girl, the peasant—live in intimate association with their Jewish neighbours. Antisemitism—that blight of Czarist Russia —is a distant, faint echo in the idylls. The world is a world of pleasant days and nights. Russian and Jew share a sensitivity to the melancholy, gentle sadness of the great plains in the Crimea and in the Ukraine.

All Tschernichowsky's idylls reflect an enviable tranquillity. Even the single exception—'The Broken Spoon'—begins its attack on civilization gently. For, after all, it is natural for prisoners, the *idyllii personae* of 'The Broken Spoon', to view the world as a prison, the inhabitants as prisoners to traditions and historical facts, wisdom subject to senses, psychology fettered by meteorological and environmental factors, free will chained to cause and effect. This becomes a breathless indictment of cosmic dimensions. But even this harsh tirade is preceded by the good-natured, detailed account of the mending of a spoon and succeeded by the melancholy chant of a socialist song.

Tschernichowsky created moody, brooding landscapes in the idylls. Frequently, he described them at such length that they were easily detachable as independent poems. Thus, the lovely vignette of domestic bliss in 'Baruch of Mayence' first appeared as an independent idyll in *Visions and Melodies*.[8] In its later setting, in the lurid plot of 'Baruch of Mayence', it gained in colour and depth. The togetherness of the Jewish family, the unmarred love of husband and wife were accentuated by the total annihilation of the individual and the community in the crusading zest of misguided Christianity. And the whole poem was strengthened structurally by the inclusion of the idyllic fragment. Similarly, in 'Circumcision', Tschernichowsky captured the melancholy mood of the Russian *steppes*. And the lengthy passages describing that mood and those *steppes* is an independent poem.[9] But it also gains as a complement to the joyful fulfilment of a hoary rite. And the orchestration of the whole poem is richer than it would be without the famous passage.

From his earliest years of creative endeavour to the very end of his life Tschernichowsky cultivated idylls. Most of them were written during his student years in Heidelberg. But some antedate while some postdate those years. Poems like 'Charms of the Forest'—so close in inspiration to the idylls—owe much to Mendele who was sensitive to the natural beauties of the Russian landscape. Tschernichowsky was conscious of his debt to

8. See *Ha-Tizkeri 'Od* in *Ḥezyonot u-Manginot*, pp. 26–9. In the final version—as it appeared in the Schocken edition—Tschernichowsky deleted two distichs and made a few minor changes.

9. See the Schocken edition of Tschernichowsky's poems, pp. 149–150.

the elder contemporary: he had dedicated 'Charms of the Forest' to Mendele. He also owed him his style. For he did for Hebrew poetry what Mendele had done for Hebrew prose before him: he enriched it with talmudic idiom. Thus Tschernichowsky became the very personification of a paradox. Although he was the most biblical personality in modern Hebrew literature, he employed post-biblical Hebrew to depict the lives of his rural characters in Southern Russia.

Towards the end of his life, he produced an idyllic poem unique in its blend of scientific facts and poethic figures. 'The Golden People'.[10] It was a bold effort to interpret life in non-mythical terms. It probes the origins of prehuman existence, but dwells with special fondness on 'the golden people', the bees, who are merely exemplars of human behaviour; the cruel laws of the beehive and the mating flight of the queen-bee are duplicated in the wars of nations and the flights of love and imagination. Against the background of the highly organized, almost totalitarian society of the bees, the poet paints the friendship of Father Anthony, a bee-lover, and a young Jewish pioneer. The Russian as well as the Palestinian landscape contributes its share of charm to this poem. Thus a triple motif, richly orchestrated, runs through it; and in spite of its tedious scientific nomenclature and monotonous enumeration of mineral and plant varieties, 'The Golden People' attests to the sublime maturity of an aging poet. It was an attempt, perhaps, to embark on a new poetic course.

C. *Ballad*

THE HETEROGENEITY of the ballad is the despair of the critics. The *genre* defies definition. Cautiously, ballad may be regarded as a form of folk song. It is a narrative song, a tale in verse with a refrain as a common feature. It may be, although it need not be, a dance-song or it may be fitted to dance tunes.

10. *Ibid.*, pp. 773–858. For an interpretation of the poem see Baruch Kurzweil, *Bialik we-Tscher-nichowsky*, Jerusalem–Tel-Aviv, 1960, pp. 256–80.

J. F. Campbell defined the ballad as 'a bit of popular history, or a popular tale or romance, turned into verse which will fit some popular air'.[11] Originally and etymologically, it was undoubtedly a song for dance accompaniment. Whether the ballad originated in a group dancing and singing together or with individuals who communicated their poetic inventions to a group is a problem that will be debated as long as critics or professors of literature support the individual or communal theory of the origin of ballad, monogenesis or polygenesis or compromise on an amalgam of both.

The balladist was the folk-singer, traditionally anonymous, living in an isolated community and working with or creating oral verse-material, the folk-entertainer *par excellence*, the predecessor of his vulgarized confrère on radio and television, in the music-hall, theatre and cinema. He concentrated on action rather than character, on an emotional core rather than on a logically constructed story. This is borne out by the great thesaurus of Professor Francis James Child's *English and Scottish Popular Ballads* and by such basic collections of balladry as *Our Singing Country* and *American Ballads and Folk Songs* by John A. and Alan Lomax.

The idiom of the ballad has been adapted and assimilated to the literatures of the world in recent centuries. In England Scott and Burns, Wordsworth and Coleridge were the masters of the form. In Hebrew literature which had no tradition of folk balladry, Tschernichowsky may be regarded as the innovator and ancestor of the ballad. There is evidence that he admired the Scottish ballads; certainly, he paraphrased 'The Two Corbies' in 1896.[12] Although he preserved the frame of

11. See *The Critics and The Ballad*, Selected and Edited by MacEdward Leach and Tristram P. Coffin, Southern Illinois University Press, Carbondale, 1961, p. 261, n. 3.

12. See *Shene ha-'Orbim* in *Ḥezyonot u-Manginot*, pp. 78–9. In the final version which appeared in the Schocken edition of Tschernichowsky's poems, pp. 51–2, there are some important changes and improvements in the text. Tschernichowsky revised his poems though not as endlessly and as elaborately as his great Irish contemporary

the ballad—the worrisome concern of the two ravens with their next meal—he changed the picture. It is no longer the slain knight, abandoned by 'his hawk, his hound, and his lady fair', who will serve as dinner for the ravens, but the dying poet on a Judean mountain. The metamorphosis of knight into poet is Tschernichowsky's invention. Absence of knighthood among Jews necessitated a shift of emphasis. Yet the emotional core remains the same in the Scottish ballad and in the Hebrew paraphrase—the desolate abandonment of knight and poet alike.

About a year later, in 1897, Tschernichowsky translated 'John Barleycorn'[13] and 'My Heart's in the Highlands'[14] by Robert Burns. Though the latter poem is not a ballad, it attracted him because of the sheer simplicity of its nostalgic theme.

Original ballads are numerous in Tschernichowsky's work. Some centre around the personality of king Saul and date back to 1893 when he was a lad of eighteen, others were composed at the very end of his life. Of the earlier ballads 'The Last of the Koraita' is a sample of Tschernichowsky's heroic pose. In the battle with Mohammed's hordes in the Arabian peninsula, the Jewish tribe of Koraita has been annihilated. The last of the survivors prefers death and immortalization in poetry to escape engineered by a magnanimous friend in the enemy camp. The near-ballad on 'Mohammed' from the same period is a study in veneration. The prophet sits among his admirers in the wilderness; the immense silence is interrupted by the roar of a young lion; the prophet, unperturbed, fixes his sandal, rises and bids his admirers go in peace. But the calm, ordinary action and the calm, ordinary phrase in a threatened environment raise him to extraordinary and finely graded dimensions

William Butler Yeats. But Tschernichowsky's revisions have not been studied while Yeats's emendations have been subjected to careful scrutiny. See Marion Witt, 'Yeats: 1865–1965', Publications of the Modern Language Association of America LXXX, September, 1965, pp. 311–320.

13. See Yohanan Ben ha-Se'orah, in Hezyonot u-Manginot, pp. 52–4.

14. See Bi-Ne'ot Harim Libi in Shirim, Berlin, 1922, p. 310.

in the eyes of the admirers. He was like Moses descending from Sinai, like the angel Azriel who will come in the day of judgment, like the sun emerging from primeval chaos, like Allah himself when he created heaven and earth.

In his early years Tschernichowsky was understandably enamoured by exoticism. But he also utilised familiar themes for his ballads. 'On the Eve of Sabbath' relates in musical verse the legend of the good and the bad angel who peep into every Jewish home on the sixth day at sundown. Wherever there is peace and order and cleanliness and piety, the good angel approves and the bad angel says amen against his will. Wherever there is quarrel and disarray, the bad angel approves and the good angel says amen against his will.[15] 'Sabbath Night', an idyll according to the poet, is more like a ballad. It recreates another legend: since the souls of the damned are not tortured on the Sabbath in hell-fire, it is incumbent upon the Jew to prolong the Sabbath as long as he can.[16]

In later periods of his life Tschernichowsky created ballads of consummate beauty. 'The Negro Boy' is the story of a slave in love with Pharaoh's daughter and echoes the biblical story of Joseph; 'Three Crowns'[17] is a poetic rendition of a talmudic legend with an original twist: of the three crowns, the crown of strength, the crown of learning and the crown of beauty—the last is shown to be incomparable and invaluable; another rendition of a talmudic legend, *Kezad Merakkedim* (How to Dance),[18] prescribes the form of dancing before a bride and sings, in Tschernichowsky's version, of a reborn Jewry in its homeland by virtue of toil and Torah.

But of special significance are the pain-laden ballads of martyrdom.[19] That polarity—heroism and helplessness—fascinated Tschernichowsky and dominated his entire *oeuvre*. He ransacked the pages of Jewish history and extracted from them

15. See *Shabbat* 119 b.
16. See *Sanhedrin* 65 b.
17. *Abot* 4, 13.
18. *Ketubot* 16 b-17 a.
19. On martyrdom in the poems of Tschernichowsky see the sensitive essay by Jacob Bahat, *Kiddush ha-Shem be-Yezirato Shel Tschernichowsky, Mo'znayim* XVII, November, 1963, pp. 432–7.

numerous poems which illustrate his antithetical concept. Again and again he returned to the Crusades and the unfathomable and, to him, incomprehensible attitude of Christian to Jew, of man to man. And he lavished all his poetic tenderness on the suffering individual. Worms, the seat of medieval Jewish scholars, famous for its ancient synagogue which the Nazis destroyed, and for its ancient cemetery which they desecrated, had an almost symbolical significance for the poet. It was the first city on the Rhine to suffer the impact of crusading slaughter. And to that city Tschernichowsky turned his poetic skill in 'The Wonderwall of Worms'—the story of a pitying wall that receded and hid a pregnant woman from the unpitying hands of Crusaders—and in the seven awesome 'Ballads of Worms'[20] which were written immediately before his death. For the Jews of Worms suffered during the Crusades and during the Black Death in 1349 and during the days of the Second World War. But Worms or Dortmund, Germany of the Crusades and the Black Death and the Nazis, Poland and the Ukraine in the seventeenth century or Russia in the nineteenth and twentieth centuries—all such cities and countries had only one meaning for the Jew: suffering relieved by merciful death. Tschernichowsky gave a new interpretation to Jewish martyrdom. Dying is not senseless but rather the prelude to a life of dignity which is being built with the blood of meek and rebellious and even blasphemous martyrs—as in 'Baruch of Mayence' and 'The Dead of Dortmund'.[21] These two poems are, incidentally, violent indictments of medieval Christianity. Although the first was finished at the very beginning of the century, in 1902, and the second after an interval of thirty-five years, they read like two chapters of a bloody story-in-verse.

20. On the sources of the 'Ballads of Worms' and on possible echoes of the legend of Pappus and Lulianus in the ballad 'Candles for the Anonymous' see S. Eidelberg, *Ha-Balladah Nerot ha-'Almonim le-Sha'ul Tschernichowsky, Bitzaron* XLIX, November–December, 1963, pp. 115–16.

21. The word Dortmund, spelled in medieval Hebrew chronicles טירמוניא is misspelled and mispunctuated in the Schocken edition, p. 615: סימוּניָא.

The past received garish illuminations from atavistic factors in 'Baruch of Mayence' and from sadistic realities of Nazism in 'The Dead of Dortmund'.[22]

Tschernichowsky cultivated three forms of poetry with masterful hand and heart: the sonnet, the idyll and the ballad. The simple structure of the idyll, the elegant structure of the sonnet, the artless amorphous structure of the ballad were his favourite media thoughout his life. Even poems which are not marked as idylls or ballads approximate to that form. Thus *Be-Erez Ephraim* (In the Land of Ephraim) is a ballad which, at a later period of life, re-interprets a main motif in Tscherni-chowsky's poetry, namely, the conflict of Canaanism which is pagan, physical exuberance, and Judaism which is prophetic, spiritual exuberance. And into longer poems he often injected an idyll or a ballad which may easily be detached from their context. Detachability, in fact, is a characteristic feature of Tschernichowsky's technique. Thus, in his last testament to beauty, 'The Golden People', he has created 'The Ballad of the Hive', perhaps his finest achievement in a difficult *genre*. In trochaic couplets, immaculate in their rhythmic precision, he has written the immortal love-and-death story of the lover of the queen-bee. Though Maeterlinck had preceded him with a skilful and quasi-poetic account of the encounter of bee and queen-bee, Tschernichowsky surpassed the Belgian mystic in sheer vitality and consummate realism.

22. On the historical background of 'Baruch of Mayence' and 'The Dead of Dortmund' and on the thematic interrelation of the two poems see S. Eidelberg, *Ha-Yesod ha-Histori be-Shirat Tschernichowsky*, *Hadoar*, January 4, 1963, pp. 162–3; on the sources of 'Baruch of Mayence' see also Meir Bosak, *Le-Mekorot Baruch mi-Magenzah*, *Mo'-znayim* XVII, November, 1963, pp. 442–4.

Chapter 5

IN A MINOR KEY

A. *Children's Poems and Tales*

CHILDREN, poets, primitives share a delight in a world of imagination. For them there is no dissociation of the real from the unreal. Animals behave like humans, humans like animals. Inanimate objects are alive and astir with purpose which often maddens the unpoetical adult.

Throughout his life Tschernichowsky felt a keen kinship with children. And he believed that 'those little ones understand more than we imagine, and know more than we surmise. ... Observe the attitude of animals to children: they still seem to understand each other'.[1]

Tschernichowsky published children's verse in numerous periodicals which were designed to attract the youngest readers. An innate childishness characterized all of them. They did not talk down or sing down to children, they did not sentimentalize their world. They endeavoured to captivate them with an immediacy of perception.

The children's poems by Tschernichowsky are brief and melodious. They lend themselves to quick memorization and to individual or group singing. They depict situational difficulties and they resolve them with happy endings. Thus, in the poem *Ha-Gannan ha-Ḳaṭan* (The Little Gardener),[2] the rabbits do their mischief in the vegetable garden; they eat up the cabbages and flee—forewarned in the nick of time that the vengeful dog is on their trail. Another poem struggles with the helplessness of the tot who fumbles in pronunciation.[3] The child-

1. *Kitbe Sha'ul Tschernichowsky* VII, p. 74.

2. See Tschernichowsky's collection of children's poems which were illustrated by Nahum Gutman and published in Berlin under the title *He-Ḥalil*, Tel-Aviv–Berlin, 1946, p. 6.

3. *Ibid.*, p. 34.

Saul Tschernichowsky and Isaiah Chernichovsky, a relative of the poet

Ms. of the first page of the story about David Kahana in the Library of the Hebrew Teachers College, Brookline, Massachusetts

ren's poems never fall into the trap of sadness. They are bracing
to the point of exuberance and ecstasy.

It is also a remarkable fact that Tschernichowsky's children's
poems are Jewish to the core. They celebrate Jewish holidays
and they capture the mood of Jewish daily life. They sing the
glory of Jewish customs. They even judaize nature. Mushrooms behave like a veritable Jewish community in pre-
bolshevist Russia. They have their internecine wars, their class
distinctions, their 'pious women' and their clever scholars.

Animals also behave like Jews: they recite grace after meals
and psalms to cure the sick. In the solitary children's story in
verse *Ma'aseh bi-Ze'ev Ben Ze'ev* (Story of a Wolf, Son of a
Wolf)[4] Tschernichowsky relates the adventures of a young
wolf in search of a cure for his father's stomach ailment. He
makes friends with a fox who leads him to a bat who advises
consultation with demons. And so the road leads to the miracu-
lous city of Istanbul, the abode of spirits. There the eldest of the
demons advises a visit to the flea—the magician who knows all
cures for all ills. But the flea does not readily divulge his
secrets. He must be made to laugh so as to open his mouth
widely and he must be given sleeping pills. Only then does he
reveal his authentic knowledge. The young wolf does what he
is advised to do. The flea prescribes a concoction made of
crab's eyes and soap bubbles tied with a crimson-coloured
strap, twenty nails, the rims of a barrel, a cock's voice, a door's
squeak. All this must be well-ground and then well-baked
with the addition of a belch, a yawn and quinine. This remedy
proved helpful, and the convalescence was celebrated with a
party where food and drink and such delicacies as *Kugel* were
served to all who came.

The story of the wolf is delightful nonsense: the episodes are
few, the plot moves with swift incongruity, the animals are
humanized to the point of absurdity. Of all the Hebrew poets
who have attempted children's songs or poems or stories—
Bialik, Shneour, Shlonsky, Anda Pinkerfeld-Amir and Leah

4. *Ibid.*, pp. 41–57.

Goldberg—only Tschernichowsky could have written the story of the wolf. For he had the innocence and artlessness of a child.

Tschernichowsky's performance in prose never equalled his power of expression in poetry. It is no surprise, then, that the eight children's stories in the little book *What Was and What Was Not* are distinctly inferior to the children's poems. They show—like most of Tschernichowsky's work—a fine knowledge of the farmer's life, a deep insight into the animal world and a keen power of observation. They play—with tongue in cheek—parlour games or outdoor games with Jewish customs. And they imitate such perennial folk-forms as *Eḥad Mi Yode'a* (Who Knows the Significance of One) which is recited at the Seder. Once—and once only—is there true artistic achievement: in the story of the spider. That little killer thinks that the gardener's hut, the king's palace built on its ruins, the central pillar that remains after the sack of the palace—all these exist for him and for him only. The whole world turns around the spider's axis. The whole world satisfies the spider's appetites.

This tale of haughtiness and egotism is designed, perhaps, to create a feeling of disgust for everything that is self-seeking and self-centred in the world.

Tschernichowsky's wife, not an unprejudiced witness, once said of the poet that he had a golden heart. He never asked for anything, he never complained about anything.[5] His poems for children reflect the gay world of the child, the world of birds and stars, animals and plants, flowers and lakes. They are as tender as the melody of a flute. And hence the name of one of Tschernichowsky's collections of children's poems: *He-Ḥalil* (The Flute). The children's stories include realistic and imaginative tales with a quasi-historical background. Hence the title: *What Was and What Was Not*.

B. *Drama*

TSCHERNICHOWSKY had a predilection for the strong men in Jewish history. Bar Kohba, the leader of the last revolt against

5. See Klausner, *Sha'ul Tschernichowsky*, p. 62.

Rome (132–5), was his hero. In a youthful poem he complained about the injustice to the 'Son of a Star' (*Bar Kohba*) who was called by an ungrateful people 'Son of Falsehood' (*Bar Koziba*). He hoped that future generations would erase that infamy, that a people 'cleansed from the mire of exile', would rehabilitate his name and his fame.[6] Indeed, he set out to do so in later poems and, especially, in the one and only play he ever published in his life, *Bar Kohba*.

The first act sketches the general atmosphere of discontent which preceded the revolt. The first scene reproduces the talk of anxious men and women, the second and the three subsequent scenes present a forgotten Jewish festival, the fifteenth day of Ab with its merry wooing of girls. Roman soldiers who intrude with less than innocent intentions are quickly rebuffed. Some of them are killed. And the first to strike is Simon, the future leader of the revolt. It is a weak first act: no characters are drawn, no people—except Simon—are named. Boys, girls, soldiers, old men, young men, women comprise the *actus personae*. Simon appears as an individual toward the very end of the act. In ten brief lines he exhorts the young men to rob the soldiers of their arms and flee to the mountains.

The second act takes place in the house of the sage and the scholar who is universally revered, Rabbi Akiba. The pros and cons of the revolt are argued with vehemence. The sages are against it, only Rabbi Akiba and his wife Rachel are for it. But even Rabbi Akiba is assailed by certain doubts. He is fortified by Rachel who has an unequivocal faith in her people. It is in their house that Simon assumes the leadership of the rebellion. The three main characters in the second act are finely drawn and contrapuntally orchestrated—the wise sage, disappointed in the undisciplined people, the monolithic wife, and the youthful rebel, endowed with attributes of leadership: love of his people, hatred of the oppressor, faith in victory and resolute will.

6. See *Le-Nokah ha-Yam* in Schocken's edition, pp. 121–2.

The third act—as the previous acts—lacks dramatic tension. The revolt proceeds, in accordance with historical facts, through victory to doom. Simon, the leader, shows firmness in his dealings with the treacherous Samaritans and gathers strength from his love for the Samaritan girl, Habibah. Both she and her father are well-drawn characters in a drama which is not over—rich in real people: she in her divided love for Simon and for the Samaritans, he in his overt innocence and covert wiles. Simon's victories gain him Akiba's unreserved support, and the sage recognizes him as the Messiah, the Redeemer, the King. Akiba's re-interpretation of a well-known talmudic legend[7] throws a new light on Pharisaic Judaism. Three out of the four sages who entered Paradise suffered physical or spiritual damage. Akiba entered in peace and left in peace because he possessed what was lacking in their faith: a great love for their people, their land, their law.

The doom comes in the fourth and fifth acts. Habibah almost murders Simon who senses the inevitable defeat in his besieged fortress—in Betar—and comforts himself with the presumed admiration of future generations. There is a marriage of blood and iron 'between him and his people, an external covenant, the covenant of Saul and Mount Gilboa . . . Betar and Bar Kohba'.[8] He dies by his own hand for under the Romans he would not be able to live in freedom nor die in freedom. Akiba is captured by the Romans.

The play *Bar Kohba* is written almost entirely in the metre of Greek tragedy, the iambic pentameter. But it is doubtful whether that is the appropriate rhythm for a Hebrew tragedy. It is certain that Tschernichowsky had a predilection for iambs and used that prosodic device effortlessly.

As a dramatist he was neither a realist nor an avantgardist. He wrote a conventional play, but inexperience of the craft

7. *Ḥagigah* 14 b. For the meaning of the talmudic legend see Gershom G. Scholem, *Major Trends in Jewish Mysticism,* Jerusalem, 1941, pp. 51–2; *idem, Jewish Gnosticism, Merkabah Mysticism and Talmudic Tradition,* New York, 1960, pp. 14–19.

8. *Kitbe Sha'ul Tschernichowsky* V, Berlin, 1932, p. 129.

produced lifeless monologue and dialogue. Fortunately, he was aware of his limitations and avoided playwriting.

Bar Kohba cannot be considered a failure; neither is it a brilliant success. Tschernichowsky had meagre dramatic talents and he never developed them to the high degree which he reached in his lyric and epic poetry. Even the four dramatic translations—Shakespeare's *Macbeth* and *Twelfth Night*, Molière's *Le Malade Imaginaire* and Sophocles' *Oedipus Rex*—cannot claim immortality. They are among the inferior products of his muse.

C. *Stories*

BOTH major Hebrew poets in this century, Bialik and Tschernichowsky, wrote a number of stories which did little to enhance their literary reputations. And both used autobiographical material. Bialik did, indeed, manage to create three stories of durable worth: the delicate reconstruction of his childhood days in 'Aftergrowth',[9] the tender love story of a Jewish boy and Gentile girl in 'Beyond the Fence' and the sturdy projection of a peasant-like type of Jew in 'Aryeh the Strong'.

Tschernichowsky's stories first appeared in various periodicals, and were immediately disappointing. The book of six stories, published in Berlin in 1922, the stories in the sixth and seventh volumes of the collected writings (1932), and the book of thirty-three stories, published in 1941, embarrassed all serious critics. Had they not been written by a well-known poet, they would have passed unnoticed or been dismissed. For they displayed neither incoherence of the avant-garde variety nor depth-psychology nor conservative, simple realism. Yet they have their place in the canon of Tschernichowsky's writings. For most of them are thinly disguised or undisguised autobiographical sketches. As such they furnish details, half-known or unknown, for the life of the poet. And

9. A representative selection of Bialik's stories in English translation by I. M. Lask was published by the Jewish Publication Society under the title *Aftergrowth and Other Stories*, Philadelphia, 1939.

for that reason alone the uncollected stories should be brought together in an additional volume.

Three in the collection of six stories complement the idylls and describe the same locale: the rich, south-Russian earth on the borderline of the Ukraine and the Crimea. And they seem to be the raw materials which have not been moulded into verse.

Thus the stories *Ashkenazim* (Germans) and *Nitpardah ha-Ḥabilah* (The Bond Was Severed) centre on the poet's birthplace and its neighbouring villages. And although they somehow escape the artistic transformations of similar material into idylls, they enhance their background. 'The Germans'—the German colonists in the Crimea—are described as being dull and precise but excellent as customers for the Jewish storekeepers. Among the gentiles who fill the pages of Tschernichowsky's idylls they are somewhat exotic. But, for the Jew, they also share the mystery of otherness in common with the Russian peasant.

'The Bond Was Severed' could have formed, perhaps, a chapter of the idyll 'In the Heat of the Day'. It is the story of a young Jewish boy's infatuation with a piglet. This is a dangerous theme for a Jewish poet. Hence, perhaps, the relegation of the material to a less conspicuous place in his *oeuvre*. What Velvele felt for the doves and the pigeons, Fishke felt for the piglet. Perhaps, the mutual affection between the boy and the 'unclean animal' was merely transformed in the idyll into the love-relationship between Velvele and 'the clean fowl'. In the story and in the idyll the boy is taunted for his strange infatuation: in the idyll, good-naturedly, in the story, both good-naturedly and angrily. In the idyll, however, the plot is outlined with a poet's art and compassion, in the story there is merely a pathetic account of a relationship. And the *deus ex machina* ending of the story does not enhance its artistic value. It is, perhaps, the price the poet paid in conforming to the traditional Jewish attitude. After an extended absence from the village the boy meets the piglet now grown into a full-sized pig—a stinking, dirty, disgusting pig. And he hurries away from the encounter—broken-hearted and disappointed.

Many of the so-called stories in the two volumes of Tschernichowsky's collected writings are brief essays or feuilletons or
ephemeral reactions to contemporary events. The best hark
back to the days of Odessa and form a series: *Odessa she-Metah*
(Odessa That Died).[10] Others have written books about the
cultural importance of that city: Rav Tzair and Jacob Fichmann.[11] But they concentrated on important literary figures
of the Hebrew renaissance. It was their ambition to enshrine
forever that Southern Belle—as the city was called—in the
annals of Hebrew letters. Tschernichowsky set himself the
modest task of characterizing some minor literary and scholarly figures. But he often achieved more than Rav Tzair or
Fichmann in their weighty volumes. For he had a good eye for
the weaknesses of individuals as well as the people as a whole:
the scholar's striving for immortality in a footnote, the vengeful
scorn for the really talented by the half-talented, the tender
attachment to the dead who, when alive, had been honoured with
utter neglect. Only rarely did Tschernichowsky write about
the literary figures who made Odessa what it was—the Wei-
mar of Jewry in the last two decades of the nineteenth and the
the first two decades of the twentieth century. His essays on
Lilienblum, Frug and Mendele are too episodic, too anecdotal
to illumine their work and their worth. But they shed an incidental light on the young Tschernichowsky who was neither
awed by the giants nor displeased with their human frailties.
In an early realization of his own future greatness, perhaps, he
had a natural, unencumbered attitude to the great of the present.

Some of the essays on Odessa are not without humour. The
wooing of Isaac Joel Linetzky, a minor Yiddish writer, for the
sake of Linetzky's beautiful daughter, is full of the impish
frivolity which characterized young Tschernichowsky. The
pettiness of petty scholars—their far-fetched hypotheses and
their jealousies—are caught by Tschernichowsky with indel-
ible accuracy. Thus David Kahana, self-taught scholar and

10. See *Kitbe Sha'ul Tschernichow-* nowitz), *Masseket Zikronot*, New
sky VII, pp. 157–225. York, 1945, and Jacob Fichmann,
11. See Rav Tzair (Chaim Tcher- *Ammat ha-Binyan*, Jerusalem, 1951.

authority on mysticism, was anxious to offer Tschernichowsky a subject for 'a grandiose poem' on condition that the poet indicate in print: 'this theme I received from David Kahana'.[12] It is a pity that the fine essay on Joel Engel, the composer, does not appear in any of the collections of stories by Tscherni-chowsky. It was there that he observed: 'one hour of original work is better than fifty years of criticism on the works of geniuses'.[13] And it was there that he contrasted—in a passionate plea—the great contribution of ignorant Jewry to Judaism with the exaggerated contribution of the learned Jewries of Poland and Lithuania. Such an essay deserves to be included in any future edition of Tschernichowsky's works.

The story *Yelag be-Bet ha-Sefer le-Mishar* (Judah Leb Gordon in the School of Commerce)[14] is, perhaps, the most significant story in the collection of thirty-three stories. It is a true incident from Tschernichowsky's student years in Odessa. At a school celebration in honour of the well-known Russian fabulist Ivan Andreyevich Krylov (1768–1844) Tschernichowsky was asked to recite two of his fables. Since other students were to read the fables in translation—French, German, and even Greek—he volunteered to read Krylov in the Hebrew translation by Gordon. After some deliberations, the school authorities permitted the bold youth to read them in Hebrew—in the presence of the bishop, the mayor and high education officials. And that was an event of no small import in Czarist Russia.

There is even a story from Tschernichowsky's days of exile in Istanbul: a rather pathetic story of a bird that died in a cage and was tenderly buried by the poet in a garden-plot in the city of minarets which the poet described as 'candles burning before Allah and spears directed at the enemy'.[15] There is also

12. See *Kitbe Sha'ul Tscherni-chowsky* VII, pp. 189–92.

13. Saul Tschernichowsky, 'Joel Engel', *Ha-'Olam* XVI, April 4, 1928, p. 269. On Engel's melodies for Tschernichowsky's poems see Menasheh Rabina, *Tschernichowsky*

be-Musikah, Mo'znayim XVII, November, 1963, pp. 450–1.

14. See Saul Tschernichowsky, *Sheloshim u-Sheloshah Sippurim*, Tel-Aviv–Jerusalem, 1941, pp. 96–102.

15. *Ibid.*, p. 102.

an indication in this story that the poet continued with his translation of the *Iliad* in Istanbul.[16]

Many stories supplement our knowledge of Tscherni-chowsky's medical career from his student days in Heidelberg to his professional activities before and during the First World War in Czarist Russia and after the war in communist and anti-communist Russia, in Germany and in Palestine. They are not without a certain charm. They tell of days gone by, of rural Russia and quaint peasants, of beatings and drinking bouts, of troika-drives through endless plains, of nostalgic days and evenings and nights. They tell of cunning types, of stingy types, of impertinent types; and, above all, of people who are non-heroic, fearful, ready to resort to any stratagem to save their own skins. They also tell of the poet's frustrations—his unsuc-cessful attempts at employment in Russia and in Palestine, his impotence in the face of anti-semitism in his native land and his deep disappointment in the face of indifference on the part of his own people. Most of them are fragmentary memoirs rather than stories. Few of the stories belong to the realm of pure fiction, and these are the worst of a poor lot. A number of them contain some extenuating remark or common sense observation like the story *ba-Refesh* (In the Mire):

> An adolescent commits his first sin out of curiosity, out of lust, out of frivolity, out of an abundance of vitality, out of leisure, out of inebriation, out of shame before friends who have already tasted the forbidden fruit, out of assurance that there is nothing to fear and nothing to lose.[17]

But as works of art, the stories warrant little serious considera-tion.

D. *Science*

THE writer-cum-physician or physician-cum-writer may com-prise a powerful combination, as the examples of Somerset Maugham in England or William Carlos Williams in America

16. *Ibid.*, p. 106.   17. *Ibid.*, p. 114.

attest. In Hebrew literature there has been a long tradition of the physician-writer syndrome from talmudic until recent times. The mutual interplay of the two callings provides a fascinating subject of study, and any serious evaluation of Tschernichowsky must consider the influence of medicine and the natural sciences on his work.

The father was an amateur veterinarian, a fact documented by the poet in his mock-serious poem 'An Occasional Veterinarian Was My Father'.[18] There is no doubt that the predilection of the parent and an idealist attitude to the art of healing determined the choice of a career whose influence may be discerned in the poetry and prose alike.

There are pharmaceutical terms in the poems and stories of Tschernichowsky. There are catalogues of terms—botanical and geological—in 'The Golden People'. And they are as burdensome on the poem as the scientific tracts in verse which medieval versifiers produced for the instruction and amusement of their learned clientele. In Tschernichowsky's case, the tedium is alleviated by his medical and poetical curiosity about the body: a contagious, consuming curiosity, which the reader cannot help but share.

Many of his stories refer to his medical career. They are concerned with patients and doctors and hospitals. The scientist fed the poet from the beginning of his career.[19] At the end of the nineteenth century Hebrew literature suffered from a dearth of terms in botany, in zoology and in medicine. Tschernichowsky ransacked the sources—ancient, medieval and modern—for useful terms or he coined them himself. He was the first to invent Hebrew names for many varieties of mush-

18. The Schocken edition of Tschernichowsky's poems, pp. 716–723.

19. The key to 'the gates of the world of Tschernichowsky' is not the fact that he was a physician as Dr. D. A. Friedman argued in his article *Ha-Meshorer we-ha-Rofe'* in *Ha-Rofe' ha-'Ibri* XVII, 1944, p. 129. For a more balanced view of the importance of medicine in Tschernichowsky's writings see I. Mishael, 'Shaul Tschernichowsky Among his Brethren' in *Ha-Rofe' ha-'Ibri* XXXVII, 1964, pp. 240–2.

rooms, flowers, grasses and trees. He was the first to coin names
for many species of birds and animals. And he was the first to
introduce pharmacological and medicinal terms—his own or
those of others—into his stories and poems. The many articles
on scientific terminology which he published in dailies, in
periodicals and sundry collections—in the Berlin *Sefatenu*, in
the Palestinian *Ha-Arez and Leshonenu*, in the New York *Ha-
Rofe' ha-'Ibri*—have undoubtedly added a new dimension to
his creativity. They deserve to be collected into a volume and
studied with the care and attention which is lavished on other
aspects of his personality.

Just as Tschernichowsky the scientist intruded into the
poetry, the poet intruded into his scientific articles. In a characteristic utterance he prided himself that he could distinguish
'between birdsong and birdsong'. And he added:

> I understood the gay chatter and the sharp twitter of the
> starling. I understood the abrupt call of the swallow between
> *Minḥah* (afternoon prayer) and *Ma'ariv* (evening prayer); I
> understood the pleasant invitation of quail from the standing
> corn in the evenings, the chirping of the sparrows interrupting
> each other . . . the trilling jubilation of larks in the sky above
> the wide expanses of the fields from early spring to the late
> snows, the mysterious call of geese, urging each other on in the
> heavenly paths when they fly north in the spring and south at
> the end of summer . . . I knew the voices of the cackling hen
> and the gander, the scream of the peacock and also the croaking
> of the frog singing with devout abandonment and longing
> around fountains and on the edge of a dung-pit.[20]

Similar passages can be found in talmudic and midrashic
literature. In modern Hebrew literature they were virtually
non-existent before Tschernichowsky.

With extraordinary sensitivity he also approached the world
of plants and flowers: 'Names for flowers were certainly invented by Eve when she plucked some of the most brilliant
specimens in order to adorn herself. . . . I set out to observe

20. See Daniel Persky, *Le-Darke   Ha-Rofe' ha-'Ibri* XVII, 1944, p.
Signono Shel Tschernichowsky in   137.

flowers which are most known to us, those that appear first
with the passing of winter ... and charm us imperceptibly on
the crossroads, on every heap of refuse, near a broken fence, on
the edge of a grove. ... '21 And like a conscientious poet with
the touch of a botanist he catalogued flowers and invented
names for them—not systematically, but in the order of their
sprouting and blooming in the land of his love, Russia. And,
on the broad bases of the scientific term and the folk-term, he
would coin an appropriate Hebrew term. As a poet he lavished
his loving care on the aesthetics of coinage. For he was anxious 'to preserve the spirit of the language, *the soul of the term.*
... '22 And he succeeded in that enterprise more than any
other man in his generation.

The crowning work of his scientific contribution was the
medical dictionary, or to give it its full name the *Dictionary
of Medicine and Allied Sciences* which was published in Jerusalem
in 1934. For many years Dr. Aaron Meir Masie (1858–1930), a
distinguished physician and linguist, had collected materials for
a medical dictionary. First as a member, then as president of
the Committee for Hebrew Language, the predecessor of the
Hebrew Language Academy—he had occasion to contribute
terms to medical and natural sciences. Hundreds of his coinages
have become lingual currency in Israel.

For many years Masie collected terms from manuscripts and
books, common and rare editions. But he died before he
finished his task. Tschernichowsky was entrusted to order and
edit the 60,000 terms which Masie had collected. The result was
an indispensible dictionary which lists the terms in Latin,
English and Hebrew.

21. Saul Tschernichowsky, *She-
mot ha-Ẓemaḥim* in *Sefatenu* I, ed.
J. Klausner, Jerusalem–Berlin, 1923,
p. 114.

22. Saul Tschernichowsky, *Keẓad
Bore'im Terminologiyyah 'Ibrit* in
Sefatenu II, 1923, p. 16.

Chapter 6

TRANSLATION: EXERCISE IN
SELF-DISCOVERY

THE TRANSLATOR is a traitor—say the Italians. But he is
also the indispensable dispenser of an alien culture. And he
plays a stimulating role in every literature—though he is the
most underrated and underpaid functionary in the realm.

No other Hebrew poet translated so profusely and so
steadily as Tschernichowsky. And no other Hebrew poet was
better equipped for the work. Tschernichowsky's massive
knowledge of languages afforded him access to many cultures.
He mastered Hebrew, Greek and Latin, Russian, Ukrainian,
Serbian and Old Slavonic, German, Yiddish, French and
English. And—with the exception of Yiddish and Ukrainian—
he used his lingual equipment to good advantage in translation.
The Babylonian *Gilgamesh* and the Egyptian hymn to the sun
by King Akhnaton and the Finnish *Kalevala* he did not translate from the original. Such was his love for language that he
regarded a thorough knowledge of the language and a cultivated mind as prerequisites for original work. Although he
fully appreciated the poetic prowess of such a man as Burns, he
rightly argued that those who aspire to gain a foothold on
the Hebrew Parnassus 'have no right to be ignorant'.[1]

In his translations Tschernichowsky neglected neither lyric
nor epic nor dramatic poetry, neither ancient nor modern
poems. Even Persian and Georgian poems were grist for his
translating zest. Sometimes he translated a few lyrics of poets
like Burns and Richard Dehmel and Ivan Bunin, sometimes a
solitary poem of Shelley or Francis Thompson or Alfred de
Musset or José Maria de Heredia or Pushkin or Tegner. Although he was not a dramatist, he was drawn to the great

1. See Tschernichowsky's verdict   duction of *Yedi'ot le-Yedide Genazim*
as literary judge in facsimile repro-   II, 1963, p. 13.

dramatic literatures of England and France and ancient Greece. *Macbeth* and *Twelfth Night* are among his poorest performances in translation. Entire scenes have been shortened and inadequately rendered. *Le Malade Imaginaire* by Molière fared somewhat better. And Sophocles' *Oedipus Rex* was the play most congenial to his idiom.

Epic poetry, so close in inspiration to folk-poetry, exercised the greatest attraction for Tschernichowsky. Apart from the Babylonian fragments of the *Gilgamesh* epic, the Greek *Iliad* and the *Odyssey*, he also translated Longfellow's *Hiawatha* and *Evangeline*, Goethe's German epic *Reineke Fuchs*, fragments of the Icelandic *Edda* and a Serbian epic, the ancient Slavonic epic *The Lay of the Host of Igor* and parts of the national folk epic of Finland, *Kalevala*.

Although he had no knowledge of Finnish, he was attracted to the poems which were composed for many centuries by Finnish and Karelian folk singers and which were gathered together by Elias Lönnrot in the *Kalevala*. For his translation he used the trochaic, four-beat line. He had acquired much experience in that metre when he translated Longfellow's *Hiawatha*. Longfellow had, himself, been influenced in the choice of metre by a German translation of *Kalevala*. And he used it with skill although not without a certain metric monotony.

Tschernichowsky may not have been aware of the brilliant researches of Milman Perry on Yugoslavian reciters of stories in verse. And he may not have known Albert B. Lord's adaptation of Perry's techniques to the epics of Homer—the discovery of the formula as a chief vehicle of oral literature and formulaic expression as its chief characteristic.[2] But he was sensitive to folk creativity. And he had the soul of an ancient rhapsode: a deep respect for the traditions of the people and a love for its formulaic phrases. Small wonder that his crowning achievement was his translation from the Greek, especially his translation of Homer. That translation alone would have secured his place in Hebrew literature. For it inured the Hebrew

2. See Albert B. Lord, *The Singer of Tales*, Harvard University Press,   Cambridge, Massachusetts, 1960, pp. 30-67.

language to the hexametric line and the epic tale in verse. And though his idiom is obsolete in many passages—such is the rapid progress of Hebrew in the course of a generation—it is still readable and enjoyable. The penultimate stresses of the Hebrew words which have been superseded by Israeli pronunciation add an archaic tinge to the entire translation.

In his excellent treatise *On Translating Homer*, the English critic and poet Matthew Arnold notes that the father of epic poetry possesses four essential characteristics, 'that he is eminently rapid; that he is eminently plain and direct, both in the evolution of his thought and in the expression of it, that is, both in his syntax and in his words; that he is eminently plain and direct in the substance of his thought, that is, in his matter and ideas; and finally, that he is eminently noble'.[3] These characteristics Tschernichowsky shared, in some measure, with his renowned predecessor. That is why he succeeded, on the whole, in his translations of the Greek epics. What is perhaps equally important, although it has not been noticed even by the devoted Klausner, is the salutary influence the Greek epics had upon his original verse.

Like all pioneers in any field of human endeavour he could not escape crudities and gaucheries. But it is remarkable, in view of the fact that his translations were the first full-length translations of the Greek epics, how rarely they occur.

In his introduction to the *Iliad* Tschernichowsky complains about the difficulties of translation. The inevitable *epitheton ornans* which accompanies the Homeric gods and men, cities and ships, is a repetitive formula which serves a double purpose: it saves the poet efforts of characterization and it familiarizes the listener or reader with the object of description. In other words, it is a device which achieves a maximal effect with lingual continence. In a simple or compound-word Homer succeeds in evoking an image which, in Hebrew, must be rendered by two, three and even four words, and only in rare instances by a single equivalent. The resulting awkwardness

3. Matthew Arnold *On Translat-*   1905, p. 41.
ing Homer, new edition, London,

makes for a peculiar diction which is anything but Homeric. Out of thirteen instances in which the word ταλασίφρονος occurs in the *Iliad* and in the *Odyssey*,[4] it was translated twice by a single Hebrew word, once by two words, six times by three words, three times by four words and once it was not translated at all. This is a typical procedure which, unfortunately, mars the beauty of Tschernichowsky's translation. The stable epithet of Homer loses stability in the Hebrew rendition. Furthermore, it is either too long to be effective or, when rendered by a single word, too weak and inexact and, therefore, inadequate.

That the verses which were swollen by the expanded epithets in Hebrew did not altogether destroy the beauty of the original was partly due to the numerous Greek conjunctions and articles which could be rendered by the *Waw ha-Ḥibbur* (the conjunctive *Waw*) and the *He ha-Yedi'ah* (the definite article) in Hebrew. Space, lost by the epithet, was thus regained to such an extent that Tschernichowsky was sometimes forced to add to the Homeric line. But he was always careful to make additions in the spirit of Homer rather than introduce poetic peculiarities of the twentieth century into the ancient texts.[5]

The task of translation was not altogether fraught with difficulties. Some of the thousands of Greek words which were admitted into the Hebrew language and literature in the Hellenistic period were effectively used by Tschernichowsky.[6] Some Greek words which had no equivalent in Hebrew were simply transcribed in Hebrew characters or slightly hebraized

4. *Iliad* IV, 421; XI, 466; *Odyssey* I, 87, I, 129; III, 84; IV, 241; IV, 270; V, 31; XVII, 34; XVII, 114; XVII, 292; XVII, 510; XVIII, 310.

5. For examples of shortened and lengthened verses, cf. Tschernichowsky's introduction to his translation of the *Iliad*, *Kitbe S. Tschernichowsky VIII*, p. XXXIX.

6. *Iliad* XXI, 23; *Iliad* XXIII, 745; *Odyssey* XII, 168 and numerous other instances. Tschernichowsky was rather cautious in the use of Greek words. Wherever a Hebrew synonym was available he utilized it to the fullest extent.

רחוב 89, הדר="/ /18
o'couu
10

Dr. Med. S. CZERNICHOWSKY
Internal diseases & minor surgery

ד"ר מ. שאול טשרניחובסקי
מחלות פנימיות וכירורגיה זעירה

תל-אביב, יום 10.III/38

Rp.

14 MAR 1938

95	16338

בירושלים.

וו@לא תענך והכפב 8 מו/ס !

תאת נולא מ אכתג תאעכור תגלת מרום
הדעו /jur הריאא פל או פ.ווגל 4.III.38
ולו/ו/רו : — תרכ/ פ ו/ר ו/א תאשורר

Francis Thompson.

תאפת רבת פל, להתוlו/אl לפאות ו/ת.
פלו אגרתל ור ות פתהגא הטל , והול
תגמא שאלופפ התק/ר ו/ולו/ פ גא ות
תתרגם בכ ר'אמ, /ופ.ורח/ואה ול תרגא
גרפתא III ר/0/ו' אלק ה@ר/לב והופ ואר

לפל טטרניחובסקי

.e.x. לw/   ...

Letter from Tschernichowsky to Dr. Judah L. Magnes in the National and
University Library of Jerusalem

Ms. of poem "I've Nothing of My Own" (*Ani-Li Mi-she-li 'En Kelum*) in the National and University Library of Jerusalem

n their endings.[7] For a renascent language like Hebrew such
additions serve to enrich the vocabulary in the direction which
was begun in the Hellenistic period and interrupted with the
Arab conquests in the seventh and eighth centuries.

There is no doubt, then, that Tschernichowsky was appre-
ciably aided by post-biblical Hebrew in his translation of the
Iliad and the *Odyssey*. But he was helped to an even greater
degree by biblical language which, like Homeric language,
gave sublime expression to the sublime simplicity of ancient life.

What Tschernichowsky learned from his translation of
Homer he applied to Theocritus. The lyrics of Anacreon
inspired him from the earliest days. Indeed, an anacreontic
poem appears in the very first book by Tschernichowsky.[8] In
1920 he published a collection of Anacreon's poems in Hebrew.
Wine, women and song—the chief themes of the bard of
Abdera—appealed to the frivolous side of Tschernichowsky's
psyche. That he also tried his hand at Plato was inevitable. The
two great dialogues on the nature of love and the nature of
beauty, the *Symposium*[9] and the *Phaedrus*,[10] owe him their
Hebrew garb. That Plato was *the* philosopher for Tschernichowsky is clear from a significant monologue of Rabbi Akiba
in *Bar Kohba*: the Greek sage is credited with the knowledge
of love which the colleagues of Akiba lack.[11] Such was his love
for Greece that he even translated so-called 'Kleptic poems'[12]
of modern Greece—poems of brigands who fought the Turks
and sought national independence.

---

7. E.g. מוֹזָה, הֶקְטוֹמְבָּה, אֵיתֶר
אַמְבְּרוֹסִיָה, נֶקְטַר

8. See *Be-Iḳbot Anacreon* in *Ḥezyonot u-Manginot*, pp. 42-3. For the
translation which he paraphrased
when he was nineteen years old see
Saul Tschernichowsky, *Shire Ana-
reon*, Warsaw, 1920, pp. 56-7.

9. See *Kol Kitbe Aplaton I*, ed. J.
Klausner, Jerusalem, 1929, pp. 17-76.

10. *Phaedrus* was not published;
Hebrew version of the dialogue by a
Zevi Diesendruck appeared in War-
saw in 1923. See J. Klausner, *Sha'ul
Tschernichowsky*, pp. 155-6; 341.

11. *Kitbe Sha'ul Tschernichowsky*
V, Berlin, 1932, p. 100.

12. The Schocken edition of
Tschernichowsky's poems, pp. 731-
732.

Tschernichowsky also translated eighteen lyrics of Horace.[13] Though he could not aspire to the extraordinary virtuosity of the Latin poet, he managed to convey a sense of Roman *gravitas* in his renditions.

13. Saul Tschernichowsky, *Re'i Adamah*, Jerusalem, 1940, pp. 99–126.

Chapter 7

ASSESSMENT

IDEAS are the preserves of philosophers. Poets concern themselves, among other things, with the concretization of ideas. They achieve their ends through figures of speech: image, metaphor, simile. And they coax meaning out of metre, rhyme, rhythm, out of devices which appear under the heading 'technique' in books on poetics.

It is easy to identify the primary 'ideas' of a poet. They are usually few in number and rich in import. The main ideas of Tschernichowsky run like musical motifs through a symphony. They announce themselves at the outset of his literary career and they are richly orchestrated in his work. They do not suffer startling transformations during his fifty years of writing and publishing. They mature in intensity and expression. It may be legitimate to speak of a later Yeats or even a later Rilke, for their poetry, in the penultimate phases of their lives, underwent a sea-change. Tschernichowsky may have been born several—as are all men. But he stayed one: a monolith of simplicity.

It is not without significance that the only pseudonyms he employed were *Ya'aḳob Tam* and *Ben Gutman*.[1] The first is the well-known allusion to the patriarch in Genesis 25:27. And it may be translated—though not quite justly—as Plain or Simple or even Ingenuous Jacob—in view of Rashi's comment: 'one who is not quick to deceive'. The other pseudonym alludes to the father of the poet whose name was Tuvyah-Gutman. *Ben Gutman* is merely Son of Gutman. And Gutman in German is a good man. In a sophisticated age the pseudonyms of Tschernichowsky are acts of courage. Honesty and goodness guide his

1. Tschernichowsky also used the name of Miriam Tschernichowsky once and that of Tscherni twice but these can hardly be regarded as pseudonyms. See R. Malachi, *Yeẓirot Tschernichowsky* in *Bitzaron* V, 1943, pp. 115–16.

pen—authentic moral forces with scant authority in aesthetics.

Tschernichowsky is the only Cartesian poet in the history of Hebrew literature: clear, candid, unmystical. Yet such is the semantic load of words, especially in an ancient language like Hebrew, that clarity itself adumbrates a type of ambiguity, that intent and intensity must be wrested out of the husk of clarity through insight and comment.

One of the chief motif-ideas in Tschernichowsky's poetry is alienism. Now alienism has been the burden of Jewish existence since the days of the great diaspora in Alexandria before the common era.[2] It is, rightly, the *idée maitresse* of Ezekiel Kaufmann's multivolumed sociological study about the destiny of the Jewish people.[3] In Tschernichowsky's case it is a double estrangement: he feels like an alien among a people regarded as alien among the peoples of the world.

There is a corollary to alienism: poverty. The poet, in common with the vast masses of East European Jewry, knew the humiliation of want. And he gave poignant expression to his destitute estate in one of his many excellent poems: 'I've Nothing Of My Own'.

There is another corollary to alienism: revolt. The massive mythopoeia of Tschernichowsky is sometimes a conscious, sometimes a sub-conscious challenge to the very existence of Judaism. To reinterpret the monotheism of a people committed to an ethical stance, and to root it in pagan mythology uncommitted to anything except to the unbridled forces in man and nature—that was and still is a dangerous assault on tradition. More than dangerous, because tradition teeters on the brink of insecurity in a non-traditional and non-religious or downright anti-traditional and anti-religious world. Like his admired predecessor in the period of enlightenment, Judah Leb Gordon, Tschernichowsky regarded excessive spiritualization as an evil that must be stamped out. While Gordon ranged

2. The best account of the cultural condition of Jews in Alexandria is given by H. A. Wolfson, *Philo* I, Harvard University Press, Cambridge, Massachusetts, 1947, pp. 4–86.

3. Ezekiel Kaufmann, *Golah we-Nekar*. Tel-Aviv, 1929–32.

himself on the side of the temporal powers—to borrow a medieval anachronism—Tschernichowsky embraced the teachings of the so-called 'false prophets' who, in his opinion, were the great yea-sayers to life; the ones who preached the freedom of joy instead of slavery to the law, the gaiety of the dance instead of the ritual of prayer.

Revolt requires strength. And strength in all its aspects—physical, intellectual, spiritual—is extolled in Tschernichowsky's poetry. Weakness or acceptance of one's lot are abhorrent vices which must be rooted out if a people is to regain its dignity in liberty.

Like all major Hebrew poets Tschernichowsky had to wrestle with the past, with the vast history of his people. Unlike most major Hebrew poets who mined the twin concept of diaspora and redemption *ad nauseam*, he discovered a new 'realm of being' in the beginnings of Jewish nationhood and reinforced modern Judaism with its half-mythical past. In his naïveté he associated that Judaism with the life-building forces of exuberance, vitality, joy. In rural Russia of the last years of the nineteenth century he also experienced and exulted in a comparable Judaism: rich in innocence, in inner strength, in physical stamina. That Judaism, he was certain, would build up Palestine. Not the learned and petrified Judaism but the soulful, ignorant Judaism.

> Ignorant Judaism gave us Herzl and his followers . . . and Jabotinsky and the men of *Bilu* and the majority of *Ḥaluẓim* (Pioneers). And that Judaism will build the national home, not traditional Judaism . . . for it knows deep down in its heart that the root of its soul and the secret of its existence is the diaspora. . . . In the days of wireless and the modern tempo of life one cannot build, it is impossible to build an eternal edifice according to the *Shulḥan 'Aruk* and the later codifiers. . . . [4]

Strength and ignorance are carried to extremes in the poetry and in the prose of Tschernichowsky. They are admired, extolled, idealized—by him, by his younger contemporary Zalman Shneour and by his predecessors Judah Leb Gordon and Micah Joseph Berdyczewski. Under the immense bridge of

4. See *Ha-'Olam* XVI, April 4, 1928, p. 269.

ages, spanned by the half-mythical Canaanite and rural Russian Jewry, there was the river of Jewish blood. Thus, Jewish martyrology of the middle ages and modern times became a dominant motif in Tschernichowsky's poetry. But even this theme, hackneyed and hoary in Hebrew literature, was re-interpreted by Tschernichowsky. Instead of elegiac effusions on the misery of Jewry in lyrical verse, he created dramatic characters who shouted defiance and hurled curses at criminals who killed in the name of Christian love. And he created dram-atic scenes of such power that their anguish became the angered inspiration of his generation in search of a new freedom in the ancient land of Israel.

The pathos of Tschernichowsky rarely degenerated into mere rhetoric. Unlike any other figure in the long history of Hebrew literature he created, to use a phrase of Edwin Arling-ton Robinson, a 'poetry of the commonplace'. In the many idylls and ballads, in the many idyll-like and ballad-like poems, he dwelled on the details of daily living—on inanimate objects, on inflections of conversational idiom—with a love and with an understanding that seemed to have vanished from world litera-ture after the demise of Greece. His keen sense of observation re-stored a visual world of infinite variety to Jewish consciousness.

Bialik marks the end of a road with his attachment to a dying past and with his longing for a nationalist future. Tscherni-chowsky is the architect of the new style and the new content in Jewish life and letters.[5]

5. Bialik and Tschernichowsky: the comparison between the two major figures in modern Hebrew poetry is a favourite theme with critics. F. Lachower wrestled with it as early as 1911 in an article entitled *Bialik we-Tschernichowsky* which was reprinted in his book *Shirah u-Maḥashabah*, Tel-Aviv, 1953. Baruch Kurzweil wrote several essays on the subject and collected them in a book, *Bialik we-Tscherni-chowsky*, Jerusalem–Tel-Aviv, 1960. Fichmann frequently juxtaposed their respective roles in his *Ammat ha-Binyan*, Jerusalem, 1951, and so did Isaiah Rabinovich, in his article *Ha-Meshorer ha-Humanistan*, *Ha-doar*, October 25, 1963; compare also Eisig Silberschlag, *Sha'ul Tscherni-chowsky*, *Bitzaron*, November, 1943, pp. 82–3.

PART TWO

TRANSLATIONS
NOTES TO THE POEMS
BIBLIOGRAPHICAL NOTE

NOTE

In view of the strong musical element in Tschernichowsky's poetry, most of the translations attempt to follow the metres and rhyme-schemes of the originals. Every translator of Tschernichowsky's poems is painfully aware, however, that much of the poet's music is elusive. S. J. Kahn has worked at his translations sporadically over a period of some thirty years, and in many instances the earlier versions have been carefully revised. He has also introduced slight changes into the versions of his collaborators, with their consent, where this could be done without damage to the poems. The translations are offered with the sincere hope that they may convey to the English reader something of the quality of Tschernichowsky's writing.

I BELIEVE

Laugh, O laugh at all my visions,
   I, the Dreamer, tell you true;
laugh, for I believe in man still,
   for I still believe in you.

For my soul still yearns for freedom,
   unbartered to the calf of gold:
for I still believe in mankind,
   in his spirit, strong and bold.

Man shall rise to heights of glory,
   vanity's fetters from him shed;
the worker then will starve no longer,
   spirit—freed, and hunger—fed.

Laugh, in friendship too my faith is,
   somewhere yet I'll find a heart,
one to share my every hope with,
   feeling fortune, knowing smart.

I believe, too, in the future,
   though the day's not close at hand,
it will come—then peace and blessing
   will be borne from land to land.

My people, too, again will flower,
   on the land a breed will rise,
that will cast their chains from off them,
   see the light before their eyes.

Living, loving, working, doing,
   on the *earth* alive indeed,
not hereafter—hope of heaven,
   not content with empty creed.

A poet then shall sing a new song,
   to beauty exalted heart awake;
from my grave, for him, the young one,
   they'll pluck flowers, wreaths to make.

                       Odessa, 1892

PLANT STRANGE TO YOUR PEOPLE

Plant strange to your people, wild, alien flower,
blessed with God's light, you have not learned to cower;
your eyes, high and proud, gaze fearless and strong,
and your lips have not ceased from their vigorous song;
in the living God's temple—your generous heart—
dwells the earth in its fullness, its every part.
For your eyes see creation indwelling in all,
and your ears listen well to the sound of God's call,
who about in the infinite spaces walks,
in the chirp of the bird and the shrub's secret talks,
in the scolding thunder and surge of the flood,
in the clouds of the south-wind, and pulse of the blood . . .
How shall foes that judge you be silent—the same
whose ways you despise, ever putting to shame
their holy traditions, as an enemy might,
whose dwellings to you are so narrow, confined!
With the hyssop that clings to the wall you live,—
in the rocks, with water drops fugitive,
with the various colours, though false they may be,
a moment bright on the cloud's canopy.
Let them shake their heads and ignore them all,
for beauty you love, though they feed you gall;
they will mock your dream and the joy you are feeling,
flesh-and-spirit mummies and quacks in their healing.
For you—are the Spring, they are pits of decay;
they smell of the grave, you are brightness and day . . .

                       Odessa, 1898

BEFORE A STATUE OF APOLLO

I come to you, forgotten god of the ages,
god of ancient times and other days,
ruling the tempests of vigorous men,
the breakers of their strength in youth's plenty!
God of a generation of mighty ones and giants,
conquering with their strength the bounds of Olympus,
an abode for their heroes, and adorning with garlands
of laurel-leaf the pride of their foreheads—
masters of their idols and like unto them,
adding to the councils of the world's rulers;
a generation of god on earth, drunk
with the plenty of life, and estranged
from a sick people and tribe of sufferers.
Fresh youth-god, magnificent, full beautiful,
subduer of the sun and life's hidden truths
with clouds of song and all its treasured hues,
with seas of melody's manifold waves;
god of life's joy, its riches and splendour,
its strength and secret stores of light and shade.

I come to you—do you know me still?
I am the Jew: your adversary of old! . . .
The waters of every ocean on earth
with all their multitudinous uproar,
could not completely fill the gulf that yawns between us.
Heaven itself and the ample plains could not,
stretching, annihilate the abyss dividing
the Torah of my fathers from your adorers' cult.
Look you upon me! Because I have gone my way
farther than all others before me and to come,
in the path where man, death-doomed, must stray—
therefore I am first among those who return to you,
in a moment when I loathed death-throes forever,
my vital soul, to earth cleaving,
burst the chains that bound it.

The people is old—and its gods have grown old!
Passions suppressed in men of failing strength,
from out the cage of centuries, spring to life.
The light of God is mine! cries every bone within me,
Life, ah life! each limb, each vein cries out.
The light of God and life!

And I come to you.
I come to you, before your statue kneeling,
your image—symbol of life's brightness;
I kneel, I bow to the good and the sublime,
to that which is exalted throughout the world,
to all things splendid throughout creation,
and elevated among secret-mysteries of the Cosmos.
I bow to life, to valour and to beauty,
I bow to all precious things—robbed now
by human corpses and the rotten seed of man,
who rebel against the life bestowed by God, the Almighty—
the God of mysterious wildernesses,
the God of men who conquered Canaan in a whirlwind—
then bound Him with the straps of their phylacteries . . .

                                                1899

CIRCUMCISION
(An Idyll of Tavrian Jewry)

I
On the Way to 'Egypt'

And Rabbi Eliákim, the *shóhet*, slowly from where he was sitting
rose, and the sheets of *Ha-Zefirah* he carefully folded, caressing,
smoothing and pressing their margins. Rabbi Eliákim was very
fond of that paper, and he, every day, would carefully read it.
When he had finished this labour: the folding, the trimming,
        the smoothing,
he stood on the wooden chair, put the paper on top of the closet,
then near to his window he drew, looking outside he stood there,

thinking: the time had come to go and join in prayer—
in afternoon prayer—his small, but pious, congregation.
Silent he gazed from his window, out over all of the courtyard,
seeing his laying hens hurrying up to their dove-cote
under the angled roof, climbing the rungs of a ladder
leaned against the stable,—slowly climbed the chickens,
fluttering from rung to rung, standing and looking behind them:
seeming to think it over, whether to go on climbing?—
Only one rooster among them, that Rabbi Eliákim was fond of,
noble and very strong, his crest and beard of the reddest,
striding with powerful strides, chest held high in his strutting,
feathers long and like Turkish gold that is pale and clouded.
Chanticleer took his stand, began to crow—all at once, then,
cut his crowing short, stretched his neck and departed,
wings outspread,—thus arousing the pious Rabbi Eliákim:
Look at that rooster! What has got into him, I wonder?
Suddenly: crack of a whip, then wheels; and after the noises,
horses, a stud team; after the horses, a wagon.
The horses slowed to a halt, and from the wagon descended,
grey-haired, strong, a farmer, unbridled the horses, taking
fodder of barley to mix in the feed-trough for his horses.
Silent gazed Eliákim: What can the 'goy' be wanting?
Saw his hat—and decided: Must be from Bílivírka
(that's the name of a village, at least so the Gentiles would call it,
but the Jews, among themselves, had named it 'Little Egypt').
When the Lord, bless His Name, took a good look at His creatures,
what did He do to prevent confusion among the species?
Signs He did provide: the horn, mane, tusk of ivory;
tails for lizards, and ears long and straight for the donkey;
on the pickerel's head, cross-hatched lines; on the reindeer,
branching horns and high; the coxcomb red on the rooster;
tangled beards for the goats; and hats—for sons of 'Egypt'.
Shaped like a pot is their hat, only a bit on the long side:
seven spans are prescribed, enthusiasts add yet another.
This is the tale of the hat, in detail, the full prescription:
Want a hat, Mr. Farmer? Go then into your sheep-fold,
find a one-year-old, wool still clean and curly,

black or ruddy or brown; then to the house, to the slaughter;
cook the meat in the pot, and in its soup you can eat it
(some prefer a roast, with porridge of grits, and so forth),
and give the skin that is left to an expert tanner to work it.
Some festive or market day, then, travel to Míchaelóvka,
go into Shraga's shop—and wait. Gossip an hour there,
go to Shlomke's shop, back at least twice to Shraga's;
count yourself lucky if Berel—Berel alone!—gets your hat done.
Cost for a single hat is fifty cents, not a penny
less will do: the price has been fixed at fifty for ages.
Famous became these hats, and their village, throughout the region
from Oráychov the city, to Sevástopól on the sea-coast.
Anyone out on the road, meeting a Bílivírkan,
greeted him thus: 'How about it? Won't you sell me your hat,
    friend?'
That's been the Tavrian custom, always, and no one will change it.
And that's how Eliákim could tell where this farmer had come
    from,
but he was puzzled to guess the reason for his visit.
So he began to consider: There in Bílivírka,
whatever can be new—and I don't know about it?
While he was pondering this, into his house came the farmer,
uncovering, out of habit, and seeming to look for an ikon:
'Greetings! Are you the *shoheṭ*? I'm from Bílivírka,
Pesach sent me to bring you: a son was born to Mirka,
tomorrow's the circumcision. Here. I've brought a letter!'
'Good!' replied Eliákim—'I'll pray, and then we can travel.
Meanwhile, you'll wait an hour, rest for you and your horses.'
Speaking, he took his cane, bestirred his stumps to foot it.
Slowly he walked down the street, and his bright shoe-buckles
    glittered.
Famous, throughout the region, Eliákim was as a *móhel*;
because of his good name.—Half an hour later
Rabbi Eliákim emerged, already dressed, with a mantle
large and warm; for his wife, his heart and home—that's Elka—
ordered him: 'Take a cloak, and wrap yourself well, to the collar.
Today has been warm, I know, but later it will be chilly.

Take it. What do you care? You certainly won't be sorry.'
Out of his house went Eliákim and came to the wagon—Behold!
Filled it was with a flock: his three small, sunburnt daughters,
Sarale, Dvorele, Tcharna, only his son was missing—
the lad, between earth and heaven, in the arms of the 'goy' was
    lying,
for the latter fully intended to take this last one also.
Agleam was the face of the 'goy' just then—as for Chúneh
(After his cousin named, the one that died of the cholera.
Kóndrat the 'goyim' called him, and they had enough good
    reason:
if Gódel is called Daníla, then Chúneh by rights should be
    Kondrat!)
bright was his face with joy, laughable too, all covered
with stains of the mulberry fruit he had been greedily eating,
even his teeth were still blue, the tip of his nose and his chin too;
happy he was at that moment, for him overbrimming with
    gladness,
kicking his legs as he swung in the arms of Micháyla, the Gentile.
Micháyla wanted to clown with the Hebrew children—he mocked
    them:
'Now I'll attack you Yids!'—and lifting his whip he threatened.
Sarale, Dvorele, Tcharna, shrieking, raised their voices,
but Chúneh was not afraid, did not budge, and raising
his fist against that 'goy', seemed ready to do battle.
Silent, surprised at the lad, Micháyla kept his position,
then shook he head, and speaking as if to himself, made comment:
—'What have we come to, alas, if Jews can stand against us!'
—'He's my little hero'—answered Eliákim sweetly—
'Leave him alone and let's ride, the children enjoy your wagon.'
Shrieks again and shouts, from Sarale, Dvorele, Tcharna—
Chúneh is with them now—and the horses start in moving.
'Peace, Eliákim!' shouts the wife—'Peace to you, dear Elka!'
—'Easy with little Chúneh! Sarale, you are responsible!'
After some five minutes passed, then said Rabbi Eliákim:
—'Children, now it is time—back to the house with the lot of
    you!'

Reluctant, the daughters rose, their father's command obeying.
Chúneh was stubborn, however, grabbing the legs of Micháyla,
opening wide his mouth, and kicking hard with both legs.
But his shouts didn't help, nor his kicking legs, in this crisis:
Rabbi Eliákim was firm—and down went the lad from the wagon.
Quickly his sisters took hold, Tcharna, Sarale, Dvorele,
running rapidly home, fleet of foot, and dragging
Chúneh behind them, while he bellowed and turned his head
    backwards.
Twinkled his little feet, exposed was his undergarment,
dangling out of his trousers through a gaping hole at the back
    side,
where, not properly fastened, buttons hung loose. At that
    moment,
what did Chúneh resemble? A little lamb, a yearling,
after the ewe, his mother, when flocks go out to the meadow:
the shepherd beats his sheep, the little lambs lag and stumble,
hurry and bellow aloud, dangling their tails—dancing,
leaping on thigh and on hip . . .
                              And the jingling horses,
in a minute—are out in the fields, out beyond the last street,
running downhill—and the village houses have vanished. The
    windmill—
seen alone on its hill, its falling vanes and rising,
giant arms—from its hill, sends its farewell blessing.
Wide open spaces of steppes and pasture-lands surround them,
boundless spaces for free men, the brightness of wild things and
    noble.

And over the steppes a spirit of silent sadness hovers,
song of eternal grief, deep and dumb and bitter,
telling of worlds that are vanished, secrets of future ages,
days to come. And the sorrowful singing comes, o'erbrimming
the innermost heart with grief, wondrous, no light in it knowing,
grief that darkens all, banishing merry music,
shrinking man's heart within, tears of his eyes benumbing.
Very familiar these steppes: in tables of human history,

very distant, there, on the border of truth and legend,
shrouded is its name, in clouds of hidden wonders.
Persians fought here with Scythians, after them pursued
tribes of the Petshánians, sons of Polóvtsi too,
and shed was here the blood of Cossacks and of Tatars.
Vanished, gone are the days when the lands of the steppes were
    exalted,
oceans of green and wild grasses gleaming and spreading their
    fragrance
from the bounds of Budzák to the great sea of Caspia,
when hardy nations pitched tents on banks of streams in the
    wilderness,
curbing their wild steeds on fruitful fields and spacious.
Only their graves have remained; the high and lonely places!
Silent, from their heights, gaze the sad-faced idols,
riddles of cold stone. Impetuous brooks in springtime
swept away every trace, every shade of the hard-riding Scythians.
Winds blew and scattered the traces of the sons of Polóvtsi,
stilled forever the camps of the Cossacks, and dumb are the
    drum-beats
near gardens of Bákhchi-Sáray. Filled are the plains and the valleys
with ambrosia and dew now, and golden corn is their garment.

Slumbers the past, in the giant graves of its own mute carving.
Yet in the black, grieving nights, when scattered clouds race above,
confounded is the moon, its face like copper burnished,
sometimes gone into hiding—it seems: the ancient legends,
then, put on flesh and blood and, lo, are resurrected.
Men whose praise was their strength, from under the sad high
    places,
rise to gaze at the living world, in great-eyed wonder,
telling their tales aloud, their voices like rustling grasses,
and travellers hear their musings, and their eyes too are opened:
seeing the face of the heavens, the clouds grown black and angry,
the empty spaces, all mute, like the secret future, they mark them—
their hearts shrink with the pain! Into their hearts steals a yearning
to mount a horse and gallop, smiting his flanks as they spur him,

sweeping over the steppes, the boundless plains and the pathless,
plunging into the mist ... Then would the traveller, smitten,
lift his powerful voice, wandering from lake to river,
filling the empty air with shouts barbaric and lonely—
swans in the rushes will hear, and wolves, near the streams of the
     waste lands,
answer from shores of the ponds, wail from their dusty caverns,—
cheered will the shouter feel, at these signs of life in the distance.
Softly then did Micháyla raise his voice in singing
a simple song of sorrow, innocent, pregnant with yearning.
Simple the melody was, monotonous, artless, perfect.
Thus will the sea-mew complain on the Black Sea shores, in the
     secret
places of reed and of rush, the Dnieper rapids and sandbanks:
crying its separate cries, destitute, weeping, and grieving—
such was Micháyla's song; and his sorrowful singing
touched the soft heart of Eliákim. He heard, in the song of the
     farmer:
bitter the tears of this heart, still fresh, filled with strength and
     courage,
but feeling his world was too small, wanting deeds and adventure,
wanting a means to channel all his still-youthful vigour,
that he might find some ease, while age upon him was stealing ...
A Cossack song he sang, and before the eyes of Eliákim
rose their camps, and he shaped in his fancy a world exotic:
slaughter and strangling and flames ... and his eyes saw visions
     beyond—
generations dead, that flourished and then, like smoke, did vanish
here, on this very steppe ... remembering the tribe of Chazárim:
a Jewish kingdom, its men mighty in arms and warlike,
steeds of the plains and spears, bows and shields and lances—
Strange it all seemed to him, but his heart contracted within
     him ...
Bows and lances and weapons, maybe catapults, even—
Then the faces metamorphosed—to Eliákim now more familiar:
the Temple, the Ninth of Av! ... and his heart shrank even
     further.

But still, but still those weapons! . . . and Eliákim pondered:
If he had been here then, would *he* have been one of those
  'gangsters'?
While he examined his conscience, out of nowhere appeared
the picture of Chúneh, his son, standing up to Micháyla,
fist clenched—and Eliákim thought: When I myself was young,
tender and small like my son, would I have stood up to this
  farmer?
Truly, a new birth of spirit, its wings bearing all before it,
has passed through the camps of the Jews, presaging a new
  generation:
Zion, its lovers, its colonies . . . and every day the papers
filled with speeches and funds, Congresses . . . Rabbi Eliákim,
stirred to his heart, was afraid—hints, and hopes, and things
  hidden . . .
Something the world was seeing, exalted, and lofty, and noble,
holy, beloved indeed; but new it was, new entirely.
Terrible, too, was this newness: and who could foretell the issue?
Strange the whole thing was, and no one could tell you its future—
'Youth', and 'Áhad Ha'ám', debates and great aspirations . . .
The old—the old, alas, before the new, was ready
to fall! Yet a little while . . . and the fissures would deepen and
  widen
beneath the tottering past—and the breaches indeed were many.
Only to the eye of the flesh did all remain as aforetime.
As with the ice in Spring: let but the sun shine upon it,
and the damage is done—the ice seems unchanged on its surface,
but should you tread upon it—melted and gone completely . . .
Happy we are for the Spring, heart-sick for that which is passing—

Suddenly, the horses began to run of themselves, excited;
stopped was Micháyla's song, and the racing wheels of the wagon
clattered a lively tune: At last, there's Bílivírka!
The lights of the houses are warm, out of their windows peeping,
winking a welcome to all with abundant love and friendship;
dogs in the streets are barking, running before and behind them,
filling the air with their barks, merry and joyous their barking.

II
The Circumcision

These were the names of Bílivírka's sons, with Pesach then,
    in 'Egypt',
man and wife to the circumcision come, and these were the chief
    at the feast:
Berele Dons, and Shmuel Butz, and Beryl the tall and the short,
Godl Palant and Zalman Dov, and Shmerel, the Lithuanian
    melammed;
Rivlin, the agent from Lodz, and Alexander Mathváyitz Shlimazlin;
Joskin, the village surgeon; Mattathias Semmen, the druggist;
and Chaim ben Rav Sender the Rabbi, broad-shouldered and
    big of belly.
He, too, was a native son, casting on Bílivírka his splendour:
'This fool is one of our flock!'—thus would they glory in him.
Together with him, Rabbi Leib was butcher and cantor in
    'Egypt'—
small and thin as a board, on one leg limping a little—
and Lazar was the sexton. Add to these three yet another,
Rabbi Azriel Morónt, ruddy and long of beard,
who served under Nicholas the First, served in the Tsar's army
full thirty years, surviving great hardships and dangers;
then he returned to the Torah, the service of his Lord-Creator.
These four then were called by their names: Azriel and Lazar
    the sexton,
the Rabbi himself and Rav Leib—the four of them wearing long
    garments,
honoured they were by the people, their voices bore weight in
    counsel.
These were the 'sacred vessels' of Bílivírka's congregation.
And there were two others besides, two others of lesser importance,
their names: Chaváydir Paska, and Chivra, she that was crazy.
Chaváydir—a man tall and lean, his nose like the tower of
    Lebanon
aflame, and his eyes as well were ruddier than the wine.
Prudent and slow in his ways, he guarded the yards of the Jews,

leading—in the muddy Jews' Street, deep with refuse and slime—
    his dogs.
The names of his dogs were: Sirka, Zuzúlka, Kadóshka, and
    Damka.
His other dogs safe at home, Sirka was with him that evening,
lying spread out in a corner, his lazy eyes shut tight,
with his mouth hunting the flies that lay on his wounded ear,
flapping his tail now and then, his face an ugly scowl.
Besides standing watch for the Jews, Paska was 'shabos-goy':
extinguishing the oil candelabra, and heating the Sabbath kettle,
building the Succoth huts, and sometimes kindling the hearths.
However, in the latter line, Chivra had the advantage:
she drew well-water too, and her fee was one or two coppers
and bread. On days when the baths had been heated,
through the Jews' Street she would pass, she would carry a twig in
    her hands,
walking and crying aloud, in words such as these announcing:
'Jews, go now to your baths! Get down to the bath-house, you
    lepers!'
Both were invited this time to the inn, to Pesach's feast,
to witness the circumcision and to take part in the drinking.

A merry group it was, all of them talking, discussing;
invited to Pesach's inn, all came into the lobby,
a room very wide and high, its windows facing the garden
of apple and cherry trees, planted by Pesach's father.
The walls about were whitewashed, and in the ceiling's centre
a circle of artistic design held a hook on which was hanging
the oil candelabrum of bronze. On the walls were pictures also
of Montefiore and Hirsch, of the wise men of Israel and Rabbis.
Viennese chairs stood around the long and festive tables,
but the guests did not seem in a hurry to take their places,
rather stood talking aloud, each grasping the coat of his neighbour,
till the Rabbi grew impatient and asked the lord of the feast:
'Nu, Rav Pesach, till when?'—'Nu, nu!' answered Rav Pesach.
'A chair for the godfather here!'—and the chair was brought by a
    servant.

The face of Azriel that moment was bright and joyously gleaming:
proudly looking on, expressing imperial hauteur,
his face like a baby's was ruddy, still, with youthful vigour;
his beard was long and grey, his hair was all of silver,
falling as best it could, in curls on his massive chest.
His brows shone silver also, beetling and bushy, and bent
bow-like, they met in the middle, bounding his merry forehead.
The company, looking on, rejoiced in his splendid old age.
Thus they sat and waited for the child and for the *mohel*.
Eager eyes all were turned to the door of a second chamber
where women were attending the mother and the man-child.
Silently on its hinge, the door of the chamber opened,
revealing a lovely maiden, of not more than sixteen summers,
Pesach's eldest daughter, one of the *mohel*'s two helpers.
Tall of figure she was, yet girlhood's dew had not left her;
the lines of her sides were firm—sculpturesque and rounded,
but her neck was slender still, her arms were angular, thin.
Breasts, twin-rounded beneath, gave beautiful shape to her tunic;
her hair hung down on both sides in thick curls, black and shiny,
falling like so many snakes almost as far as her feet,
with the strength of a powerful fist, lying thick and heavy.
Lovely the maiden indeed! And the crowning grace of her beauty
was that woman and girl in her form still seemed to wrestle,
the palm now to one, now the other. Like a tender oak she was,
slender and upright and tall, in which the eye already
could see the beauty and strength of the splendid tree to be.
Her eyes were large and grey and full of a joyous radiance,
her lashes, long and black, shading the sockets somewhat.
Whenever she lifted those lashes, her glance and its light, of a
    sudden,
would pierce the onlooker's heart with delight, tender, enchanting.
Her arms outstretched, in her palms lay the child, on a cushion
of pure white velvet curled; and the girl leaned backward a little,
for her new-born baby brother was rather heavy to carry.
Slowly she stepped. And her cheeks for a fleeting moment only
flushed with embarrassment—regaining their usual calm
when she saw the face of the other *kvatter* coming to greet her.

Still, she seemed for that moment as one anointed with holiness:
'The *Shechínah*, look, on her face the *Shechínah* is dwelling!'
said Berele Dons, but the rest of the gathered guests, admiring,
said: 'May she know no Evil Eye!'—Taking the child, the *mohel*
placed him in Azriel's arms, turning to where he was seated.
The baby was large, and his skin was fresh, like a ruddy rose;
serene he lay on the cushion of velvet, white and gleaming.
Thus to our eyes at times appears the sun in Autumn,
at the end of the day, in the dusk: on plains of bluish snow
it descends and touches the edge of the field, its face a-flame.
Many they were who stood crowding, surrounding the chair in
the middle,
standing and waiting, their faces aglow with a light almost
sacred.
In the lobby of Pesach's inn, a holy silence reigned . . .

III
The Feast

Quickly the man-child was brought to his mother in the bedroom,
his voice through the house resounding—'I swear, the boy is
clever.
"Murder!" he's crying, and rightly: of his private rights they've
robbed him!'—
whispered, to Shmuel Butz, Mattathias Semmen, the druggist.
Noise and confusion again, as they all resumed conversation,
filling the lobby once more with lively discussion.
Shoved and crushed by the guests, out of the room went the
women,
Miriam's relatives, friends, familiars of the household,
joining the tables together, spreading their white-cloth covers.
Briskly and cheerfully clattered the bottles and jars as they brought
them,
setting them out in rows on the table, some in each corner.
Near them stood mountainous peaks: baskets made of crystal,
silver bowls, piled high with *chala*, jams, and wafers.
Seeing the jams and the bottles, the crowd at once was happy,

full of good will, but inclined to hang back a little. So Pesach
spoke his little speech, telling his guests with affection:
'Wash your hands, my friends, and sit at the holiday table,
feast to your heart's content on these, the good Lord's blessings.
Out in the hall you'll find a towel and pitcher of water!'
This was a speech that found favour in everyone's eyes, and they
    crowded
round the water-pitcher, washing, pronouncing the blessing.
Back to the lobby they came, sat in their places, and waited.
Rav Sender, the Rabbi, was first to bless upon the 'whiskey',
passing the honey-wafers, and, with like zealous passion,
the pious, the free-thinkers—all, followed his example:
hungry the people were, since morning they had not eaten.
Joyous their voices resounded: 'Life, Rabbi Pesach. To Life!
May we be worthy of good, salvation see, and comforts!'
—'Lord of the world, amen, on us and on Israel this blessing!'—
Very quickly the baskets and bowls of their contents were
    emptied,
and already stood in their places a host of platters—
filled with chicken livers, mashed in the fat of swans.
Roasted and done to a turn, salted and peppered, and garnished
with bits of onion—in short, the cook really knew his business;
tender it was, full of juice, its colour the shade of topaz.
Silenced the conversation, the millstones were not idle,
only the sound of forks and knives was heard in the silence.
Then came the turn of the lettuce, shredded into a salad,
spiced with bits of garlic, and onions in fat of chickens,
appetizing the mixture—it vanished, too, as quickly.
Only then, in great bowls, appeared the fish, the *gefilte*:
yellow perch, and a pike of wondrous size, enormous.
The rest of the fish were 'small fry', of all sorts, tasty and tender,
some of them roasted on fire, some stuffed and thoroughly
    cooked,
with drops of oil—like golden dew upon them sprinkled,
'highly seasoned', with radish and onion, and Turkish raisins;
Miriam was famed far and wide for her stuffed fish, and this time
luck had been with her too, her joy in the fish was endless.

In the mouth it melted, and seemed of itself to go sliding
down the throat of its eater, and sweeter than honey its bones
    were.
Along with the fish, of course, went the wine in its bottles,
old Crimean wines, a few from Israel, the 'Carmel':
they honoured the Rabbi with the last, then the others tasted it
    also,
praising it highly. Hunger appeased, and mellowed with wine,
they soon were talking again, joking, contentedly laughing.
They talked about the market in wheat, and about the famine
(louder grew the noise: in Israel we all are original),
discussing matters political, Queen Victoria's illness,
till, at last, they came to bargaining in the business
of Rothschild and Hirsch and their wills, ending with the plight
    of the workers.
Shmerel, then, the *melammed*, raised his loud voice, saying
(being Lithuanian, he was learned in Torah, though also a radical):
—'Listen, my friends, to the words of a Lithuanian *melammed*!'
Thus did Shmerel begin, and then gave a brief review
of proletarian hardships as revealed in history:
straits and famine and bitterness of hopeless oppression, the
    workers
harder than rock, however, their many trials surviving;
looking for help to the people, all 'Israel' everywhere.
—'This red wine, what is it, if not the blood of our workers,
shed—being shed!—in the fields of Zion and hills of Judea?
On your heads be their blood, if you should still keep silent
before the ICA oppression, which is bringing all to destruction.
As a gentile proverb puts it: 'Let each man give but a single
thread, there's a shirt for the poor man!'—Thus finished the
    melammed,
pale with passion his face, eyes beautiful and gleaming.
Silent the people listened, nodding their heads as he lectured,
women wiping their eyes with the corners of their handkerchiefs.
When the speaker had finished, in the silence, out of the blue sky
a platter began to circulate, and soon the sound of jingling
coins in the lobby echoed, and heavier grew the platter.

The congregation rejoiced. For every man's heart is gladdened
by helping his comrade, and Shmerel's face was sweating with
happiness.

'Well, I swear'—said Shébsili, stroking his beard as he spoke
(he had just come from Poland—they called him 'the Polish
night hawk',

since they called every Pole a night hawk, that is, a *ganef*):
'Well, I swear, this Shmerel—might be a man, if he weren't
a Litvak. Pretty sharp customer. Are they Jews? I doubt it.'

Everyone heard, and they looked at Shmerel, to hear his answer,
waiting to hear, for they knew he was clever, though a
melammed.

Shmerel shut his eyes, then, asking an 'innocent' question:

—'Wasn't our Father Abraham a Lithuanian, Rav Shébsil?'

—'What?!'—the latter answered—'How come? Father
Abraham!'

Answered Shmerel:—'It's written: And he called to Abraham
*shéynis.**

If he had not been Lithuanian, *Shayndel's* he'd say, and not
Shayne's.'

The gathered guests all enjoyed these words, and their laughter
rang, as they relished the wisdom of the Lithuanian, saying:

—'Shébsili! Why are you silent? Give the *melammed* his answer!'

'Eh'—answered Shébsili—'Pfui! Who listens to Litvaks anyway?
But tell me—I've often wondered, and never could answer this
riddle:

Ever see a Litvak bearing less than two names?

Or, if not, then surely he has two sets of *tefillin.*

Or, at least, two wives, deserted in Lithuania.'

The gathered guests all enjoyed these words, and their laughter
rang, and they relished the wisdom of Shébsili, the Pole.

*That is, 'a second time', but also
colloquially 'the son of Shayne'.
Shmerel the Lithuanian takes a
Hebrew word and plays on the fact
that in *Yiddish*, a Lithuanian might use
a similar-sounding word differently
from the way most of those in the
company would use it—there being
marked differences in pronunciation
among Lithuanian, Polish, and south-
Russian Jews. The Pole comes back
with a dig at 'radical' immorality.

Very pale grew Shmerel then, an actual case recalling;
but he conquered his anger, gave answer to Shébsili, saying:
—'Hush and listen, Shébsili; you're probably not wholly ignorant
of the *Haggádah* of Passover: why did the Lord of the Universe
slaughter the Angel of Death, who was certainly just, my friends?
Shébsili, think it over!'—and the guests in unison shouted:
'Just was the Angel of Death! The answer, Shmerel, the answer!'
Shmerel gave answer thus, speaking his piece, and saying:
—'Just was the good Lord too, the dog was to blame in the
    matter:
Shébsili, just you may be; but, you dog, who asked you
to judge—when you have no right!?'—and the guests kept
    laughing and laughing,
and Shébsili, like a chameleon, turned red and white and red,
thinking how he might answer his opponent's taunts—but that
    very
moment they gave him soup, with *kréplach*, warm and meat-filled;
and that soup had just the gleam of gold, refined and molten,
and the bright rays of the sunshine, in its bubbles of fat refracted,
were blue and red and yellow. So Shébsili thought it the right
    thing
to stuff his gaping mouth, opened to answer the *melammed*,
with three of the *kréplach*, meanwhile spilling a spoonful of
    soup—
and the quarrel stopped in mid-air.
                                Thus were they sitting and eating
soup and roasted meat: hens and swans well-fattened,
enjoying wines of Crimea, arguing, joking, and laughing.

The sun long since had set, when Eliákim sat in the wagon
and the horses moved; but this time they were not racing,
for the hands of Micháyla were weak from all the wine he had
    drunken,
and the horses were free to go, having no road, harum-scarum,
while, at every jolt, Eliákim's head was nodding.

                                Heidelberg, 1901

Here are the graves! Yours too among them!
  Only three days past
all the bloody sacrifices
  gathered here were cast.
Your body too, alas, my dove!
  No stone marks where it lies—
yet have I found you . . . and I've come
  to hide me from men's eyes.
I've come, and I shall tell you all,
  my history confide
since that awful day of horror,
  the day I died.
And I *am* dead! For now another
  man am I, abhorred—
Have you forgot that day of terror,
  abandoned by my Lord?
The clanging brass's message rang,
  the countryside astounding:
'Down with the Jews!'—from tower to tower
  the dread alarum sounding.
And in the streets the crowds of farmers,
  craftsmen, men on horses,
groans of the dying, children weeping,
  women's pleading voices;
broken vessels, clothes in tatters,
  blood in the mud like water,
shouts that fill the soul with quaking:
  'Beat them! to the slaughter!'
On their cruel, twisted faces
  livid hatred glowing,
waves of anger, seas of wrath,
  aflame and overflowing.
Amidst it all, myself . . . and then—
  the flashing knife unsated;
the thronging mob around me stood,

eagerly they waited . . .
And seeing their brutish, savage faces,
  their outstretched hands' damnation,
in a muffled voice I cried an answer . . .
  Day of consternation!
I cannot remember now those words
  I uttered in my plight—
But I remember: the cathedral,
  organ's tones, and light,
seas of voices rising, soaring,
  everywhere prevailing—
Seas of song! and impotent
  I stood, my spirits failing—
The gathered priests, the chanting monks,
  the altar's burning ember . . .
I cried an answer . . . forgotten? No!
  Forever shall I remember!
For then did I damn my people, Israel,
  my mother's breasts, my nurse,
my God . . . and what my father sacred held
  I spat on with a curse.
Then did I damn too all my hopes,
  all my being smother,
to a stranger crying: Father!
  to a stranger: Mother!
To an alien god I knew not
  vowed, no homage feeling;
to him and all his host of saints
  I bowed my body, kneeling.
Then stone idols, dumb and cold,
  on my walls were raised,
but blind they were and hollow-eyed,
  they blankly at me gazed:
'Stones are we, no heart is in us—
  greatness ours, and power,
beneath the stone soles of our feet
  stars and planets cower.

All creation quakes, and earth
  trembles, at our nods;
kneel thou, too, wormlike lowly:
  we are thy gods!'

My new gods ... ! and all at once
  before my eyes there ran
pictures of my boyhood days,
  not yet thirteen, a man.
Now first, a proud Bar-Mizvah,
  with a trembling, novice's grip,
I bind upon me the *tefillin*,
  fearful lest they slip.
For my tender soul can feel
  the kind examination
the elders always give new members
  of their congregation.
And I see my father's face,
  sparkling, bright with joy—
what thrills of awe and exultation
  tremble through the boy!
Under the yoke of Torah I bend,
  the Torah of my Lord.
None in the land like me is happy,
  and high my spirit soars.
I count thus: one and two ...
  five ... and seven turns;
the thin strap bites into my flesh,
  stems the blood and burns.
My arm aches, but my heart within
  like fish in water leaping;
tang of leather, sharp and pleasant,
  to my nostrils creeping.
'Betroth thee unto me forever'—
  But I my trust betrayed ...
'Betroth thee unto Me in loving kindness, in compassion!'—
  In alien paths I've strayed ...

'Betroth thee unto Me in faithfulness,
    and thou shalt know the Lord'—
Alas, my God, Thou hast delivered
    Thy sheep, like things abhorred,
into hands of strangers, who abuse them . . .
    My dove, at last awake?
Terrible things I'll tell you, gently;
    listen, heart, and break.
I'll whisper to you in the darkness,
    in the night dissembling,
lest your eyes see while I'm speaking,
    lips that move with trembling.
For I fear your gaze: well knowing,
    when with mine it clashes,
your judging eyes will strike, as with
    a thousand, scornful lashes.
Our darling children, do you remember,—
    those two that now are free?
I liberated both their souls . . .
    Miriam resisted me;
Zipporah, also, nestling close,
    her sister's hurt deploring,
looked upon me with those eyes
    of hers, imploring . . .
She went first . . . her tender eyes,
    I could not bear them more—
Alas, my daughters, turn from me now!
    My eyes, with grief how sore! . . .
For still that vision burns within me,
    as in my eye, aflame,
sucks my heart, consumes my brain,
    the poor strength of my frame.
Were I to weep a thousand years,
    and floods run down my face,
till my hollow eyes became like stone—
    could I that sight erase?

I am the man, the father I,
who slew his daughters, saw them die,
and did not turn his knife away,
till he was steeped in blood as they!
Before my eyes they writhed in pain,
convulsing, swallowed blood, in vain—
They wrestled with death's bitter smart,
no mercy meeting in my heart,
no father's feeling ... really dead?!
Far easier had it been instead
to feel my heart, with tongs of fire
bruised and crushed, in anguish dire ...
I doomed them to dungeons of death's night
who were made for life by the God of light,
for I could not, alas, I could not bear
my bitter fate: to see that pair
in enemy hands, in the hands of those
whose pleasure is always when blood flows;
forgetting, in homes of the enemy,
honour and holiness, dear to me,
whose price in streams of blood I've paid,
that their children, in linens well arrayed,
might come, as it were to a masquerade,
to shout in glee as they watch the game:
the roasting of Jews on tongues of flame ...

Being dead, my dove, how you are blest!
Remember the daughters of your breast?
Remember yet: at eventide,
silently dreaming, side by side,
around us a network of blue and the hush,
the lindens steeped in a secret flush,
the setting sun that lingered yet
on the tower-windows, black as jet,
but stained with a pure and golden red,
that gradually paled and suddenly fled ...
And darkness grew, a spreading pall,

and slowly there faded away the call
of the ringing bell's artless prayer
melting gently on the air,
trembling a while in the nothing of space . . .
Then, when silence was complete,
dust-clouds billowed down the street,
bellowing cows and lambs' faint bleat:
from the village pasture came the herd.

From out the eastern willows it seemed
at times that flaring fires gleamed,
and the bowl of the moon, but lately risen,
seemed caught in a flaming, bloody prison.
And the night was come, the night descended . . .
The alleys darkened, were attended
at every window with candle-light,
but the streets were still alive with night.
Before the mounting of the moon
the village grew still, was sleeping soon,
and the rising river mists spread and lay
encamped about it, thick and grey.
Peace eternal in the silence of night,
its shadow-charms, uncertain light,
its secrets, voices of mystery,
that echo near and far-off flee;
the wheel of a wagon, heaped with grain,
shrieks as it passes a narrow lane;
the voice of a dog, a voice of fear,
now heard, now fading on the ear . . .
And the former peace returns until
the earth is hushed, the cloud's shade still . . .
Silently night has come and flown.
The Milky Way has wandered down,
the Bear o'er his sons is gently bending,
bowed to the earth, with thickets blending;
among the clouds, the morning star
shines fair and graceful from afar;

the pure-gold stars dim and pale,
till, one after one, they suddenly fail;
the moon diminishes and sinks;
the eastern sky pales and pinks.
The east wind wakens a light breeze,
dew-drops wet the garden and trees,
the scent of the flowers is sharp and clean
that rises soft from the pasture green.
Movement stirs among the leaves,
and a murmur of waves in the river heaves,
from one bank to the other rolling . . .
Then suddenly, down from heaven falling,
rain jubilant shouts as of sweet-sounding voices:
a waking lark in the village rejoices.
The morning lightens, the morning wakes,
as the bucket in the well-mouth scrapes,
with movement on the beams above,
with hoof-beats that, digging the sand, run by,
and smoke that goes curling up to the sky . . .
Do you remember, dove?

And I would sit by candle-light,
sit there waking all the night,
while all the world slumbered deep,
and listen to their innocent sleep.
And sometimes standing I would stay
at their bedside; suddenly they
would murmur sleepily: some soft-whispered word,
breaking forth and fading—though hardly heard
and not repeated, it seemed to prevail,
and the father's heart in me did fail.
Exceedingly bitter my life, and woe:
who could assure me, how could I know
no enemy-death would threaten there
beside the cradles of my fair;
no strong, rude hand could harm the two,
my precious ones, while yet the dew

of childhood moistened still and fed
their pretty heads? ... and my heart would be dead ...

Our humble house do you recall?
Tumble-down and white of wall,
three windows facing on the street,
its roof where grew the hyssop sweet ...
It brought us only happiness!
And when it had grown much too small
and narrow to contain us all,
still it seemed to us like the sight,
to a brown swallow, of its warm nest
where cold cannot creep to disturb her rest—
a nest full of song and full of light.

Our tiny garden do you remember?
The breezes stealing, soft and tender,
made softly eloquent the leaves,
like one who tells secrets or relieves
heart's infinite burden, song without end,
in the graceful ear of a loving friend.
The apple tree, standing dumb;
and all the day, the quiet hum
of the bees about it, swarming bold;
each young leaf's green, and the gold
of its fresh fruits, wholly fair;
graceful acacia, standing there,
like greybeard locks the white of its blooms,
its loveliness, ere Autumn looms;
the birds that twittered, every one,
from early morn till day was done.
Beds of flowers, and lanes of sand,
beans and sesame on every hand:
when caressing breezes blow,
the beans in twisted tangles grow,
curling like radiant locks of hair;

and blood-crowned poppy flowers are there,
of every kind, all flooded with light.
And there was a corner near the gate,
where hazel and cypress cast a shade:
harvests of thorn were the chief displayed,
and our little ones came playing there
and pricked themselves, and for repair,
weeping loud, to you did run,
who, comforting, did kiss each one,
and with capable hands their garlands weft
(the swallow sang in the garden then)
from the few leaves of sesame left
after stormy nights, in our garden beds,
and put the crowns upon their heads.
Ah, hosts of such forgotten things,
each line, none missing, rays of light,
and joys of happy minutes blessed,
all gone down with them to the well,
are now upon me! without rest . . .
From the deep sea of forgetfulness rise
to stand alive before my eyes . . .
They rise and whelm me, wave on wave,
and I am orphaned like the grave . . .
But a magic light and a joyous note
is cast upon them, like a coat
of radiant brightness over all
the least bits of life that I recall.
And the gleams of joy seen once again
oppress me with a great pain
like salt upon an open wound.
O Lord, my God! is not the day
of labour not yet slept away
enough, that memory must add its bane,
bright memory, of joy and light?
Ah daughters! daughters of the pit and night . . .
Not mine the hands that shed the blood
and clipped the young and tender bud

ere it ripened in that thicket's shade,
but the enemy's hands that slaughter made ...

Accursèd be, oh cruel nation!
  Cursèd be your name;
may the curse of heaven dwell with you
  to your eternal shame!
Accursed among all mankind,
  let the malediction swell
and blight the light of day from you,
  go down with you to hell!
May your powers fail, your marrow run dry,
  with its sin your soul be cloyed,
in *you* be cursed each human feeling
  that in *me* you have destroyed!
Drown in the blood of your sacrifices,
  sink in the sea of their tears,
and each night on your couch awaking
  groans of wounded assail your ears ...
Let the worm of your remorse
  eat you and never sleep,
leech-like in your spirit rooted
  your life-blood seep!
Let the Lord hasten your destruction,
  his plagues on you decree,
till you strike terror in your *own* heart,
  from your *own* self flee!
Afflict you with all sorrows that are,
  beneath you shake earth's crust,
by venomous, creeping things despised,
  abominated by the dust!
Till you loath your very features,
  till your sight will terror raise
in all God's creatures, in your own soul,
  frightful to your own gaze!
Hell and Hades rise to greet you,
  living, may you spy them;

may your children, on your shrines spitting,
   dishonour and deny them!
The disgrace of your children, and a curse
   among all the nations,
the symbol of desolation, horror,
   down the generations!
O send, my God . . . I pray Thee, send,
   Thy sword, that Thou bereave them,
till, all revenged and utterly desolate,
   childless Thou mayst leave them!
'Pour out Thy wrath upon the nations
   that know Thee not,
and Thine anger on the kingdoms
   that call not upon Thy Name!'
For they've consumed Thy people's dwelling,
   they Jacob's portion eat—
Let Thy wrath poured out strike terror deep,
   desolation be complete!

   Fathers tell to sons:
   there are the pit-born ones,
that rise from grave-like caves, in terror shrouded;
   that thirst for blood of those
   who rest in sweet repose,
in innocent and peaceful sleep unclouded.
   And they have beaks like owls,
   these nameless creature-fowls,
and bat-like drooping wings the night-time dimming;
   and secret witchcraft lies
   in their lidless eyes,
like eyes of whales that are forever swimming.
   Their faces corpse-like pale,
   or like starved men who fail
from hunger, dusty, dark, and harrowed;
   but their two lips instead
   are like rich fabric red,
their gleaming teeth like flint are arrowed.

When wings of shadow fall
  at night-time over all
and light of day on every wall is dying,
  they then rise up and Lo!
  from out their graves they go
to lonely roads and highways, all a-flying.
  When wings of shadow fall
  and night is over all,
when wisps of clouds across the sky are fleeting,
  the trembling spirit hears
  the storm-wind sigh its fears,
its shouts the swaying forest loud repeating,—
  then, when darkness falls,
  like shadow silent crawls
the Terror where its sacrifice is sleeping,
  and with her hungry lips
  the innocent life she sips
unsated, still its blood-stream sucking, seeping . . .

Would you too, my dove, were thus,
  and with you I
could be like these blood-sucking vampires,
  lest my strength run dry!
Every night we'd rise, we'd rise
  from graves where we have sunk,
to drink the blood of these butchers
  until our souls were drunk.
Sip by sip and drop by drop,
  on the blood-streams nursing,
drunk on sorrow, drunk on groans,
  on oppression's cursing,
till my eyes would see them tremble,
  still unsated, gloating
at their gaze that froze one night of storm,
  their hair in terror floating.
Drop by drop, and sip by sip,
  sucking, pressing, nursing,

till the light of dawn we'll split
  light of joy dispersing!
Revenging thus the wells of sorrow,
  and the seas of slaughters,
suffering women, babies' corpses,
  and the shame of daughters.
Revenging thus our sanctuaries
  that their hands defiled,
all the innocent, all the pious,
  corpse on corpses piled;
all the souls deprived of life
  whom life had barely kissed;
all the hopes, the magical dreams,
  shattered like the mist.
Revenging thus an ancient hate,
  the scorning of our name,
our spirits, which in the mire proud feet
  trampling did defame!

Ah! how terrible is the dark,
  shrouded all in night.
My heart aches and my body pains,
  from the cold wind's searing bite.
But in the town—a furnace roars . . .
  See, there, bright flames leap higher!
These hands of mine have wrought this deed,
  have lit that soaring pyre—
that with it may go up in flames
  a corrupt nation's might
and sins—eternal ruins, where owls
  shall hoot in its castles' night!

From church returning, the hymning done,
  after that fateful hour,
they took me and they put me
  in the monk's high tower.
On the second day I rose

and wandered dumbly down,
drawn to everything, from one end
  to the other end of town.
Open-eyed and yet not seeing
  where my foot-steps led,
deep within me lead-like heaviness
  and all a-whirl my head,
bits of phrases and ideas
  and thoughts, all thrown together,
scattered pieces without order,
  without rein or tether,
rising, grasped, almost I could
  a wondrous pattern note,
but saw it not: like the fog it was,
  that on the stream did float.
And a giant spirit takes hold of me,
  in my bosom waking,
whispering, speaking, counselling,
  all my heart-strings taking.
It tells me what I must do now,
  lighting in me a spark,
but it whispers softly to me . . .
  silence now, and dark—
A cloud of grey, the sire of darkness,
  blankets now from me
the rays of light that might be shining
  for only me to see,
spreading over these my creations,
  making bright day night.
I could not call them, then, by name,
  try though I might—
At that moment I'd have given surely
  all my life
to know the thing that to my heart-strings
  cut like a knife;
for this I knew, I'd been commanded
  to do some thing at last,

but what it was—had vanished from me . . .
　　Thus the day passed.

A chill wind sprang from the river's shore,
　　from the low marshes winging,
the last lone chirp of a song-bird faded,
　　hid in oak-leaves singing.
A secret hand already had lit
　　the lights in the sapphire sky.
And to my room in the monk's high tower
　　sadly wended I.
I came to my tiny little room,
　　shrouded all in dark.
In judgment I stood listening there
　　to the village noises—Hark!
From far below they rose to my window
　　like sounds of a roaring river . . .
Alone I stood before my God,
　　my Rock and my Lawgiver,
high above the noisy world
　　and foolish evil's taint,
waiting for my command, I listened—
　　Till before a pictured saint
I saw a single, beckoning candle
　　flickering stand,
like a light of salvation my God had brought
　　thus to my hand.
And the dark chambers of my soul
　　suddenly were bright,
as the candle lit lamps of memory,
　　awoke my wounds, my plight.
As if life's suns and seas of light
　　were flowing from that wick
and spilt within me—such to my spirit
　　was that candlestick.
Waves of heat passed through my limbs,
　　then trembling did unnerve me;

I hurried, but my knees were weak;
   my legs refused to serve me.
My clothing in that very room
   I piled up in a heap,
and, when I threw that candle on them,
   angry fire did leap.
And on that flaming hearth I threw then
   everything in turn,
choice oil for light, and furniture, all
   that was prepared to burn.
Like little snakes that silent coiled
   with cunning laughter,
the tongues of flame rose up and burned,
   licking at the rafter.
Some minutes and the flames
   hurry, leap, and run,
return upon their tracks—and press
   together then as one,
till, eagerly and hungrily,
   they form into a wall
of pillars—that are heavy with smoke,
   and then—to coal-brands fall.
Boards of ash-wood, planks entire,
   all a deep blue-red,
reddening as bricks will redden
   into a brick-kiln fed,
and in the furnace of those rooms—
   rivers of fire part,
crackling, roaring by in streams,
   and in sparks upstart.
And lo, the sparks outspreading
   are springing wells
to spill upon the neighbour buildings
   their fiery spells.
Now a reaching hand of flame
   on fresh prey renewing

its grasp, from out the conflagration,
    now the fire forth spewing
thousands of tiny flames—and sparks
    are raining over all,
as if God's lights from very heaven
    scattering did fall,
or, like myriad giant tongues,
    in thousands did come
to lick the walls; and they
    had coloured some
with tints of brightness and of flame,
    warm and alive.
The towers—are great flaming torches
    which heavenward strive.
From the church's high-arched vault,
    lead in sheets,
by the torches melted, become one blaze
    which flowing meets—
a river whose flaming waves
    glow hot and white,
like a great, huge, hidden eye
    weeping its plight;
weeping for all the loveliness
    of delicate construction,
all the treasures of man's wisdom
    given to destruction.
Columns of smoke . . . and heavy clouds . . .
    storming lava-flames . . .
The monastery ashes, the whole city
    after it claims.
In the noise and confusion I
    ran through the street
to see my enemies' broken spirits,
    witness their defeat,
to watch and gloat over tears I saw
    flow from a father's eye,

when he heard the groaning voice of his son
  from the furnace cry.
I laughed, I laughed, in the city streets
  at the weeping dames,
when a fellow fled from his burning house,
  his coat in flames!
Our daughters then I sacrificed,
  since the altar was at hand:
I was willing and refused not
  my Lord's command.
Two perfect lambs our daughters were,
  burnt-offerings to God . . .
the first such sacrifice since Israel's people
  the Temple trod,
since from their sanctuary they were scattered . . .
  A sacrifice! our daughters—
Our precious ones were cast, alas,
  on the altar of man's slaughters! . . .
In the roaring flames . . . ah, children mine!
  Not among those beasts of prey . . .
Never!
        Now I've come to tell
  how all is burned away.
There in the city push and run
  who cannot hope or feel,
men and women like wounded groan,
  like madmen reel.
And the flame eats all about,
  to the ends of the city flees,
there our dwelling too consuming—
  and the garden cypress trees.

Beneath the eaves, beside the door,
was the nest of a swallow you had seen before,
and when snow melted, winter fled,
and days of spring-time lay ahead,

from the ends of the southland and the sea,
from the land of light, would also flee
this bird, and, with music filled,
her nest on that beam she would rebuild.
And hers was innocent, childlike chatter,
from when first the morning light would scatter
till when the shades of evening would fall
on forest trees, and house, and wall;
and she would labour all the day
to bring a twig or a wisp of hay,
to gather wool when the sheep were shorn,
or goat-hairs caught in the brushwood thorn;
and cement them with mud, and at the head
with straw and feathers would make her bed.
Then she would hunt when this was done:
flies, and crickets that sang in the sun.
She would lay her eggs and keep them warm,
and when in the nest the swallow form,
her brooding finished, first chipped through,
boundless was the joy she knew.

But when on the roof the flames took hold
the swallow's heart with fear grew cold.
Helpless she fluttered about and then
quickly hurried back again,
her trembling wings covering the nest,
she screamed for the infants at her breast,
trembling, quivering, chirping with fear;
and again she soars, for the flames are near.
Again, again, o'er the nest she wheeled—
and none to save her, none to shield!
I saw the swallow, saw her fly
through the clouds of smoke that split the sky,
into the flames. She seemed to be
one of the sparks, that had learned to flee,
spreading its wings above the glow,
protecting them thus . . . and so

she rested and ceased to call,
and in the furnace vanished all.
There were moments, moments proud,
when, deep in my heart, and shouting loud,
a ceaseless voice, like a drum, was heard—
saying: 'Save it from death—redeem the bird!
Rise, son of man, and heed those pleas!'
If I had but wanted, I could with ease
have saved that nest and the life that was in it,—
but I could not act . . . as if for a minute
my powers were gone—
                              For were you not
like to that swallow and her brood?
Who pitied you? Was not your lot,
and that of your babies, as cruel and rude?

How splendid to me seemed the memorial light
    I had bathed the night in!
To the river I went, to the river to see
    and to delight in
the sight. Night's hush and darkness
    were spread on the hill—
which weird creatures of gloom
    did with terror fill.
And like a gleaming, glorious vision
    created by magic names,
on the great black cliff there rose a palace
    of glowing flames.
It seemed to me that flowing fire
    formed into wall and tower,
and a citadel of pale flames
    did from the ashes flower,
and that, within, a torch of purple
    did roar and swell,
peering from the windows,
    as from the eyes of hell.

Why, my dove, have you come to rest
here, in the darkness of the pit?
Rise—if you could!—at my behest,
look at the light and glory in it!
Here it is cold, but there, on high,
in that other flame, our daughters wait,
with holiday singing in the sky . . .
Hurry, lest we come too late,
and fear bring tears into their eyes!
Come up, my dove—my dove, arise! . . .

Heidelberg, 1902

THE BROKEN SPOON

Perhaps the bounteous sun, upon the land,
Fades from the western skies, amid a sea
Of light and love, hangs on a parting kiss
Of glowing gold and dying radiance
With silver oaks and verdant dahlias;
Rejoicing before spring at happy pairs
Of wedded thrushes, flying across the sea;
Pouring their gold in rivers, he illumines
The leaping flashing fins that cleave the waves,
And bathes in brilliance fading azure clouds.

Perhaps he visits, before he goes, a hamlet,
Lonely and desolate, past plains and fields,
And there a quiet, forgotten nook, a garden
With flower-beds beneath the heavy shade
Of overhanging, dark acacias.
Forgetting time and change, they live the life
And dreams and sufferings of a fleeting age,
Creatures of old traditions, antique blooms;
Red, glowing poppies, scented marjoram,
With purple-blossomed crown imperial,
And climbing creepers, seizing on the fence,

Hanging their cups of white and hyacinth,
And fair-leaved bean-plants, shining pansy blooms,
Perhaps the vernal zephyr gently breathes
Across the dreary steppe—the bounteous sun. . . .
Perhaps! But when it climbs across the fence,
Spreads from the watchman's court, and passes over
The lofty wall, and pierces through the bars
Of heavy iron—then it pales and shrinks
To one small spot of golden, mournful light.
The lattice darkens, steals the little lustre
That hangs upon the nitre in the wall—
The beams are swallowed in the heavy shade,
The shadows close around the eighteen souls
Immured within that gloomy prison cell.
The eve drew near, and ended were their songs,
And each man sought his corner and his woe,
His suffering, his misfortune. But their pain
Was frozen in them, like their hearts; the sun
Could not revive them; and the light spot died. . . .

First Prisoner:
— But yet another day has come and gone . . .
Tomorrow, O my brothers, what will happen
At meal-time, when the soup is handed round?
The time is come to mend the broken spoon:
The soldiers' steps have died away outside.

Second Prisoner:
— We must inspect the 'slit' lest some one spy;
Today the 'Beak' is peering, scenting, sniffing.
Where is the ink?

First Prisoner:
— In the little bottle, wrapped
In paper, with a Latin name on it.
Long live the healing science! May it serve
To help us in our need! Doctor, what do you call
The mixture?

Third Prisoner:
                    — Potassium permanganate.

Second Prisoner:
— Long may it live! What shall we do tomorrow?
Find me a knife, a string—I shall begin.

Another Prisoner:
— Silin, where is my ladder? I'll go up. . . .

The eyes of all the company were fixed
Upon Silin. Then silently he rose,
And, with a fleeting smile upon his lips,
His chest protruding, and his shoulders raised,
He strode like a returning conqueror,
Approached the stove, and waited for the other.
Then hastened to him from the watching group
A red-haired dwarf, with clear and sparkling eyes.
He leaped upon his shoulders, and he stood
With outstretched hands, and seizing with his left
A jutting ledge, he opened with his right
The chimney door, for therein were concealed
The prisoners' treasures: 'hay', a pen, a knife.
The dwarf, amid the loving looks of all,
Took from the cover of the stove the knife.
For dear it was to them, and all the pain
Of keeping it. (Forbidden to the prisoners
Were knives, tobacco, writing-instruments.)
Simon the warden took them, and he sat
Amid his watching comrades, in a corner.
Thus did he mend the broken spoon: he made
A row of little holes, all parallel,
Upon each section. Lightly did he turn
The knife between his fingers, and he drove
Its sharpened point, until it pierced the spoon
And reached the other side. A slender cord
He threaded through the final holes of both

The columns. Then he drew the ends together
And crossed them, and he passed them once again
Amid the holes, and so throughout the row;
He pressed them well, and firmly joined the parts.

A Prisoner:
— That work is good which has with it somewhat
Of friendly conversation—and no less
Because we lie immured. Come tell me, gentlemen,
How came the first of prisons to the world?

The company divided in its views.
'It was a king'—'A lord';—till one replied:
'A child and butterfly, both free and merry,
Frolicked together in a sunlit field.
The child, rejoicing, gathered sheaves of corn,
Cleaned them and hurled them from him many times,
Till he grew weary—and he found the blooms
Of beautiful, blue cornflowers, but alas,
He picked them in excess—they did not please him.
He met the butterfly, more lovely far
Than sheaves of corn or cornflowers, and he sought
To catch it. Long he chased it unavailing
Until it flew into a hollow tree,
And then he covered the opening with a leaf;
And when he wished to look upon his prey,
He moved the leaf a moment—and his heart
Yearned for it till he could not leave it; so
He watched that butterfly until—it died.
And great ones saw and learned to do as he.'

Another Prisoner:
'The first of worldly prisons was not built,
It was created by a word. When God
Made heaven and earth, he made the greatest prison.
The world and all its fullness—but a gaol,
A vast and narrow house, both wide and stifling.

All creatures are incarcerated there
In chains of lead and brass; beneath the yoke
Of old traditions, caught amid the toils
Of tales of a forgotten generation,
Fettered with laws of being and creation
From nothingness, amid the primal mists
We stand upon the threshold of destruction;
Resentful of the code of craving stomachs
And fruitfulness cut off. We are immured
Within that prison; Will is sick and weak,
Shackled to bones and veins, and Wisdom slave
To sensuality, and minds and nerves
Restricted but to heat and cold and food;
Beauty time's bondman, Nationalities
But orders of climatic types; Free Will
Dying in chains of cause and circumstance;
Truth sacrificed to state and industry,
And Faith, in captive bonds, dragged at the heels
Of infidel development. The first
Of worldly prisons was not built, it was
Created by a word!'

Third Prisoner:

                              'O happy he
Who has descended to the matter's depths. . . .
The spoon is finished! Cease, philosophers!'
He poured in water—not a drop was spilled.

The faces of the prisoners lit up.
Astounded at the labour of his hands,
They sat in silence, and the silent walls
Closed in upon them, wondering, as they heard
The prisoners' chanting in the cell above:
'Come, let us leave this old and weary world,
Shake off its dust. . . .'

                                        Melitopol, 1907

SHE-PILGRIM

On narrow paths, the little kid I nursed has come with me,
  and my basket carries mountain flowers from thorns of Galilee;
the young men set their caps at me, whene'er I ask, whene'er I
    speak,
  and I seem to them a thrush flown down from Hermon's snowy
    peak.

Though insulted, I refrain—Why should I let my anger through?
  If I believed them—I'd be laughing ... Beating heart, would
    that I knew:
whether I am laughter's butt because I've come from Galilee,
  or am I fairer than my playmates? They are mountain maids
    like me.

We are dark, and we wear homespun; no Canaanites reach our
    home,
  our valleys there are fenced with rocks so few can go or come.
But the lowland girls are dainty, fair, and ogle their desire,
  they have broidered robes from Egypt, salves from Sheba and
    from Tyre.

I am dark, as are my tresses, bound with lilies from the steep,
  for the mountain wind has tanned me, and the night frost
    bitten deep,
since the sun of Spring descended to each brook and garden-bed,
  till, when Autumn touched the heights, vanished goat and
    oxen tread.

Golden dust—from pilgrims' herds—billows all around,
  rising, palm-like, in the distance. With song the vales resound ...
I know not what my grief or gladness: Is it for love I'm sick,
    I pine,
  or remembering our heart's gladness—David's sanctuary divine?

1909

DEATH OF TAMMUZ

> ... and behold, there sat the women
> weeping for Tammuz. (Ezekiel, 8:14)

Go forth, Zion's daughters,
and weep ye for Tammuz,
for Tammuz, the bright one, Tammuz is dead!
Days of untimely Autumn and agonised souls,
days of gathering clouds and eclipse, lie ahead ...

At the break of dawn
in the brightness of morning,
let us rise to the thicket more black than the night,
to the grove lying hid among visions and secrets,
to the high-place of Tammuz, the altar of light.

What dance shall we dance,
encircling the altar,
what dance shall we dance for Tammuz today?
Turning right, turning left, step seven and seven,
let us kneel and bow down to him: 'Come ye back, pray!'

To the right, to the left,
step seven and seven.
Steady, unswerving, and slow—hand in hand!
Let us all go forth then to seek for Tammuz,
youths alone and maidens, each in their band.

On the main highways
sought we for Tammuz—
at the fork of the roads, sunk in sun and in light,
that are pleasant and peaceful and warm to the heart,
the swallow there dipping, the sparrow in flight;

in narrow lanes stretching
through fields of tall grain,
sown thickly, with poppies and thistles that cling,
by the fountains' clear marges and murmuring rushes,
where reeds in their spring-time and green sedges sing;

over fissures and gullies,
to the river descending,
over shrubbery and ditches, and through the weeded vale ...
O winds making game of the grasses, give answer!
O turtle-dove, partridge—spied ye his trail?

We sought for Tammuz ...
at the fall of the leaf,
in the forests of cypress, where the sumach-tree grows,
lest, drowsy, he slumber in scents of the cedar,
of odorous mushrooms, in circling rows.

We sought for Tammuz—
we found not Tammuz!
Went down to the valleys and mounted the hills,
went out on the trails of all mysteries, wonders,
all places that living divinity fills.

Then saw we: the thicket
and Ashérah—are fuel,
about the grove's secrets—consuming flames leap ...
We hear but the pleas of soft, hungry nestlings,
round about the altar—a white marble heap.

And the cataracts where,
we were once wont to say:
the water-sprites magical charms would repeat,—
now summer's returned, roots of rushes are parched,
grind teeth then and whistle at the havoc of heat.

Not a trace do we find
of the meadows' demons,
for, with the wave's secret, their laughter fled too;
the meadow—a pasture for cattle, and he-goats
dance to their troughs at the fall of the dew.

Go forth then and weep,
Zion's daughters, take heed,
of the woe of the world, whence wonders have fled,
ah, the woe of the world, eclipse of its soul:
for Tammuz, the bright one, Tammuz is dead!

Mikhailovka, 1908

TO THE SUN

Our fathers when they were in this place, turned with
their backs towards the Temple of the Lord, and their
faces towards the east, *and they worshipped the sun towards
the east.* (Sukkah: Ch. V, Mishnah 4)

I

I was unto my God like hyacinth, like mallow,
that in its world has naught but this its bright sun,
and an angel urging it: 'Come grow, little blossom, burst
into your song of rejoicing, sing in the biting nettle!'

Then I sucked the damp of ploughed soil. Over me like wine
this scent of fertile earth passed, over her tender clod.
Does He lack for father and priest in the city-sanctuary,
that He has brought me here and made of me His prophet?

Shall I value the pitch on the bark of the silver cypress
less than this your precious oil, that gilds the head,
and treasure scents of the pear tree and of the field I have guarded

less than spice of Sheba's pedlars, than my incense and nard?
To you I kneel in silence. I bow in delight you to honour,
and like a golden ear in a cornfield heavy with grain.

II

And like a golden ear in a cornfield heavy with grain,
   that with much beauty rose and climbed with all its might,
   like this single ear that hides its secret in its bosom,
a pledge of eternal life, slight relic of long ago;

like an ear from ploughed earth stolen, sucking the village's breast,
   wet with a vital sap, dreaming the dream of its splendour,
   so did I too grow! But my soul is thirsty still.
Day follows day, alas! Shall I redeem the pledge?

My dream has not yet come! My path is hid from my eyes.
Turning about—perplexed: What have I, who is mine . . .
   Have I reached the border yet? Or is it already passed?

Did my father lie to me, will he not keep his word?
I, budding grain am I, and my father my sun is mine,
   who mountain mists commanded me, warm rains did me ordain.

III

He mountain mists commanded me, warm rains did me ordain,
   twilight of depths of the sea, where a great silence dwells,
   and a thick cloud of flame, over its crater burning,
before it bursts skywards, out of the earth's confinement;

and tables of stars too small to contain their numbers,
   the sun with hosts of ocean-flames upon his back,
   and secrets from eternity, that father learned from father,
traditions of simple villagers, caprices of sick city-dwellers,

that I might be axis and essence of his world, by him fashioned,
centre of all its centres, abundantly treasured
   for the present and the future, and for the vanished past.

And, all the grace to increase, he stinted me not his colours.
  He made me very rich—to the measure of his strength, which
    is mighty—
with symphonies of light and shade, of scarlet, blue, and red.

IV

Symphonies of light and shade, of scarlet, blue, and red,
  embalmed in crystal cold, sleepers in aquamarine,
  living the momentary life of a hot scattered spark
within heavy-coloured porphyry and the hidden wakes of ships;

and patterns of wood-veins in boards of mahogany,
  and blood-soaked trees that powerfully stream,
  and colours before the dawn and of evening awash in blood,
that, dropping golden treasures, never will grow poor,—

one melody are they, one wondrous song, exalted.
  Is the joiner of numbers the one to solve the riddle?
  Or will you, biology's scholar, tell to me the secret?

Simple hearts long since have solved it; and I too
  from the simple heart have learned, for my heart has not
    deceived me!
  I knew the woe of each age, was charmed by each nation's song.

V

I knew the woe of each age, was charmed by each nation's song:
  the dream of Egyptian wizards, their hieroglyphs drawn on
    walls,
  and writings of the druids, stamped in stones of chalk,
amulet on parchment, magic song—stammering poor.

And in lines commanding ages and nations gone before me,
  in spells of shepherds whispered on thresholds of their folds,
  in dithyrambs uttered by soothsayers with their writings rapt,
and in talismans of China—in these my curious glance

discovered but this prayer, the plea of flesh-and-blood:
'Thou-That-Art in the secrecy of Being, preserve for me the blood,
  extinguish not Thy fire, kindled in me by Thy mercy,

fire aflow, preserving fire, one spark from Thy Flames!'
That is the great summation, lodged in the bitter heart,
voices of souls wrapped in light, or lost in alien dark crying.

VI

The voices of souls wrapped in light, or lost in alien dark crying,
  contend within me, for I not enough have made myself holy.
  A borderland, merely a doubtful-doubt, a doubtful-certainty,
surrounds me like a dream with multi-woven caprices.

And with perversities of the living who cling to each judgment
      attacking
  Judgment, as I strove to undermine the Almighty Shaddai,
  I wore the armour of innocent trust over my uniform
and in daily secularitics my remnant was very small.

Were it not for the scents of a fat, crumbling clod of earth,
choking heat that scatters with the chaff from the granary,
  sound of a ploughshare's cleaving and a singing scythe in the
      corn,

all these absorbed by me in the village, in my freedom and prime—
who would stand by me in trouble, in battle, when shrank my
      heart,
  as I stood between the living and the already dying?

VII

As I stood between the living and the already dying
  (how terrible my calling!) with scalpel sharp in my hand,
  now weeping out of joy, now cursing in my wrath,
I took in the last light from a strange dying eye.

To the thunder of powerful guns rolling in the meadows,
   to the fire in my trench's dark shining for me alone,
   I noted the last line, the living erased from my page,
as from a bejeweled threshold a precious stone is plucked.

And yet in that very spark of the dimming eye,
   in that light absorbing light and not yet blinded forever;
and yet in that flash of fire, that wounds as it burns, in that fire

   summoning fire, commanding persecutions and terror,—
you were in them; and this your majesty did confound me;—
Had I come too soon, or perhaps my Creator had waited too
   long?

VIII

Have I come too soon, or perhaps my Creator has waited too
   long?
   'Gods' are all about me, filling all existence.
   Stars are my gods, to which I pray—I am charmed
by your presence, by the light of the day and the pallid moon.

For besides you nothing is, O sun that has warmed me!
   You are children of sun to me, cocoons that hang on trees.
   Children of sun—the elephant tree and peels of garlic,
light and heat metamorphosed—as in the seething charcoal.

All Life is a voice of prayer, the prayer-of-All:
to you cry jackal-mothers when they litter their cubs,
   to you sing battle trumpets in the camp at dawn,

and the suns in the higher sphere, when swept by prayer's voice.
   I sing in infinity's choir and I shall not be silent:
   in my heart abides the dew on Edom's fields still falling.

IX

In my heart abides the dew on Edom's fields still falling
   and moistening the holy sands of the desert of God;
   and in my ear lives the song, that comes when shadow falls
and a tender star is kindled to ancient melodies,

and night-primeval's wings cast darkness on the world,
   and the secret of the desert and the night are joined as one,
   and from their tents the assembled tribes on every hill now turn,
and bow to Him with trembling in their joy and their misfortune.

And though the nation has changed its skies, the skies of blue,
though the sight of its stars is darkened, and it suffers in the yoke
   of heavens foreign to it and still turns backward and forward,—

yet once in each month it goes out in the night of mystery
to bless this very moon, just as it blessed it then
   on the peak of the Mount of Mounts, where the eternal God is
     dwelling.

X

On the peak of the Mount of Mounts, where the eternal God is
   dwelling,
   in clouds of light appears a giant with fiery Law!
   Before his radiance sinks Chaldean Bel on Euphrates
and features of the Sphinx on the red-channeled Nile grow pale.

In his hand a staff, to shatter gods—and dumb is grown
   the pride of Zeus, who gives life to marble, at his Word
   Perún flees to the woods, and the moth and the worm meet
on the breast-plate of the Libyan priest, and make Wotan's trees
   their prey.

And then, when times have changed, the East grows light again—
Abashed are Ethiop's idols, ashamed are Ormazd and Cherub
   and idols of Arabia before the light of the Crescent.

And still the vision ... an age, as one in a crucible trying,
   shall create its God to come—and we'll worship Him with
      song—
for my heart moves me to sing to Orion and the sun.

XI

For my heart moves me to sing to Orion and the sun—
   Shall you be judges against me and set me in the dust,
   because I do not pour my wine to the mass's God,
nor set on His head a wreath, with public dances?

For in His heavenly Temple, without picture or parchment,
   in the beauty-of-all in All, His Cherub answers me not,
   nor did He come to blind me with His Book of Ancestry proud,
signed according to law as a foolish pledge.

But if over you waves should pass of inspiration holy
and a joyous trembling during creation's act prophetic,
   with a wealth of life of heart partaking of all things secret;

   true in the pride of your love with a strong man's charity—
by Him then you are accepted, like a garden of gifts
when the fruits of the trees ripen and the bean plant pods.

XII

When the fruits of the trees ripen and the bean plant pods,
   when the wild weeds grow, and all breachers of bounds and
      hedges,
   when the grape-seed ripens in the grape-skin's bosom
and rays of light are hidden and, filtered, are treasured;

something of them will be kept till epochs end, when the climates
   of this land are metamorphosed and faded the scent of her woods,
   with remnants of houses on pillars, fugitives from decay,
with graves of nations' rulers, with urns and amphorae.

And after thousands of ages, come out from a narrow pit,
it will shine on peaks of towers in courtyards of every prince
   of worshippers of fire, in bonfires raised by maidens;

and will burn in the brain of the greatest genius, and in the flesh
of the singing mosquito, and in the hollow generation lacking
   gods of a vanished world—who seize me, I cannot escape.

XIII

Gods of a vanished world seize me, I cannot escape!
   Gods of this nation which beautifies all who know its touch,
   Beauty became its Wisdom, and its Wisdom was Beauty,
showering from its loveliness on Hades and on Ocean.

I am charmed by the sea's north-winds from among the trees,
   that tell of the frost which covers all with agate patterns;
   and among strong pillars of the sun, and in temples I have
     explored,
this light I have imagined, that wills to recur within me,

but a spark from the East it is, preserved by me from Canaan;
   Dan's graven images claim me, tamarisks filled with trembling,
Ashéroth, lumps of rock, I worshipped in Chaldean Ur.

Which way shall I choose, and where is the path for me?
   Shall I pour my oil to God, or shall my choice be of Zeus,
or an image of the last age in the kingdom of *idols*?

XIV

An image of the last age in the kingdom of idols,
   or a song of a dream of strength we shall establish forever.
   For the eyes of man will test and discover the secret of matter,
compounds of delicate atoms within the gold and the tin.

And from the inanimate turning he will trace a line and path
    to the kingdoms of the trees and of the hidden plants.
    One single chain is his: fungus found in stains,
green moss of the marsh, the almond, and the elephant's young.

And the secret of heat will be grasped, electricity and light,
mysteries of magnets, of the flowering of a barley-grain,
    a live nerve's trembling, which strains without release,

    and all will become one secret, the secret of secrets—Life.
The song will be sung then to him: My sun it is that warmed me,
I was unto my God like hyacinth, like mallow!

XV

Like hyacinth, like mallow, I was unto my God,
    and like a golden ear in a cornfield heavy with grain;
    and mountain mists he commanded me, warm rains did me
        ordain,
symphonies of light and shade, of scarlet, blue, and red.

I knew the woe of each age, was charmed by each nation's song,
    the voices of souls wrapped in light, or lost in alien dark crying,
    as I stood between the living and the already dying;
had I come too soon, or perhaps my Creator had waited too long?

In my heart abides the dew on Edom's fields still falling,
on the peak of the Mount of Mounts, where the eternal God is
        dwelling,
    for my heart moves me to sing to Orion and the sun.

When the fruits of the trees ripen and the bean plant pods,
I cannot escape, I am seized by a vanished world's gods—
    or an image, in the kingdom of idols, of its last age not yet done?

Odessa, 1919

THERE WAS A KING IN ISRAEL

There was a king in Israel
  'mid elders gathered there,
who wielded still his weapon
  on a mountain high and bare.
There was a king in Israel
  on a mountain high and bare.

There was a king in Israel
  did many servants share
who plied well at the spindle,
  and one was wholy fair.
There was a king in Israel
  and one was wholly fair.

She used no oil or ointment,
  and perfumes did despise:
desire was in her stature,
  radiant were her eyes.
She used no oil or ointment,
  radiant were her eyes.

There was a king in Israel
  whom Philistines did defeat;
he armed his skilful warriors,
  went forth the foe to meet.
There was a king in Israel
  went forth the foe to meet—

as he swept down, forgetting
  the praises of his name,
his palace and its jewels,
  his treasures and his fame;
as he swept down, forgetting
  the praises of his name.

A vulture swooped—he marked not—
   and, striding over the pit,
one only face remembered,
   saw eyes that love had lit.
A vulture swooped—he marked not—
   saw eyes that love had lit.

He knew there was no returning
   from the way he went with a sigh.
Too old he was for loving,
   but young enough to die.
He knew there was no returning,
   was young enough to die.

1918

THIS BE OUR REVENGE

In memory of the Ukrainian dead

Our blood will yet be revenged! Not in vain
have the drops of holy purple moistened the earth!
No ear drinks in the anguish of the widow,
no eye takes note of the raped one's bitterness,
nor is there a comforter for the babe—
yet there is revenge!

We are small and weak! We shall not go up
against you with axes, cleaving women with child
(as you do), we shall not burn above you
the roofs of your houses, nor with iron rods
shall we crush the skulls of infants,
while yet your strong hands have not uprooted,
while yet your unclean palms have not erased
God's likeness which hovers over us,

the marks of ancient spiritual nobility
and the treasures of dedicated generations
which we have gathered up for the hearts of humanity,
fragment by fragment, in flashes and sparks,
through hundreds of lifetimes and ages,
erected through abstinence and consecration
under the yoke of our Ten Commandments.

Not us need you fear, nor destroy! Do not tremble
at the band of dogs our flesh has fattened,
at the pack of wolves you have fed with corpses
in the thickets of your pleasant woods.
Your vales, splendid with velvet grasses,
the greening spaciousness of your plains,
the standing grain of your fields, enveloped in gold,
fallow fields covered with thorns and aftergrowth,
and the distances of your roads and cross-roads,
your fragrant little gardens—
each and every spot where our corpses fell,
pile on pile—our strangled, our slaughtered,
those very pits into which you cast us,
like so much refuse and dung, human-beings
bound, to be buried there alive,—
if these should bring forth blooming rose bushes,
and blushing crowns of fragrant pinks,
ruddy mallow and glowing poppies—
these would not speak, these would not speak to you!

Their embroidered carpetry steeped in blood
would not bear witness to your deeds,
but serve as garlands on the heads of your mistresses,
the abundance of their colours would decorate your flags,
and make vivid your victorious banners.
Us do not fear,
rest at peace, hounds of blood!

And yet—
our blood will penetrate within you
and poison the very foundations of your being,
sucked up by your eyes, cold as jackals,
your hearts more hard than millstones,
your every limb, your every vein;
spreading through tissued fibres of your muscles,
till your every cell will answer softly—
like the echo of an echo . . .
but you shall not know!

Day by day it will fill you with its poison,
day by day more cruel, hard of heart.
Each corpse you will add to the myriad others
will strengthen you to add yet another,
each new sigh that your deeds will waken
will drown the one that went before . . .
But you will not understand—
till the day of our revenge will come,
the day of retribution!

Till the measure of your crimes is full . . .
and you pour all the venom of serpents in your heart,
and the well of your spreading poison,
the stench filling your soul,
emptying them out all about you,
for the fruit of your loins to inherit—
then comes the Judgment Day!

The day when the curve of your knife shall be stuck
in the throat of your brother, the son of your mother,
as if slaughtering in the yard or village square
your choice pig for Easter eve,
and to your eager ear his dying groans
will sound like song and holiday.

Day of revenge!
The day when your son shall pluck your beard turned grey,
threaten you with his hard fist,
and deep from a human-beast's throat
shall call you: Villain!
In the full sight of the congregation crying.

Day of revenge and retribution!
When exposing herself, like a brazen bitch in her heat,
drunk with beer and stammering,
your beloved daughter shall tell you
of her adulteries . . .

That shall be our revenge!
May our revenge live on—
bequeathed from generation to generation!—

                                        Odessa, 1920

THE GRAVE

In memory of the Ukrainian dead

There are many like him there—unsymbolled heap,
    against which the ox will trip that treads the wheat
and the farmer curse in anger as he ploughs;
    his skull is a mound, or grasshoppers' retreat,
before the Autumn—only the clouds will weep
    cold tears for him, the storm still him with scorn—
They alone will grieve; for no son will find the path
    to him, nor 'Father!' cry, nor praying mourn.

The years roll on and level out his grave,
    which wakens from its sleep all sown with tare;
the wind's in the whistling sheaves that o'er it wave;
    but, in the dust, that hapless one rots there,
knowing not why he is furrowed or a mound,
or why he lived, or timeless bit the ground.

                                        Odessa, 1921

SAUL'S LOVE SONG

'And there ran a man of Benjamin'—that was Saul
(I Samuel, 4:12, and Rashi's commentary)

I

The Women:	Bring us to the stillness of thy garden,
	for we are come to see thee, O fair one:
	Let us smell thy clusters of henna,
	thy plantings drop spice, and thy savours
	are Edens that make us drunken:
	We have gathered thy myrrh and have gleaned
	thy good spikenard in the bed of spices;
	we have plucked from among thy mandrakes,
	from among lilies and roses:
	Where aloes grew, we have played:
	We have been mischievous beside a garden-fountain;
	on the hair of our heads are the glittering drops
	we have sprinkled each on the other:
	We are weary, our legs are weary:
The Beloved:	Pray turn ye, my dears, to the cool place:
	For, lo, the heat is great,
	the sun is a consuming flame;
	there, curtains cover the walls,
	a breathing coolness restores the soul,
	and ivy vines will shade us:
	Rise ye, my dears, let us go:
The Women:	We have eaten thy honeycomb with thy honey,
	we are sated with nuts and sweet cakes,
	thou hast garnished sponge cakes with apples:
	We have drunk of spiced wine
	and the juice of thy pomegranates:
	Let us see the dresses thou hast sewn,
	examine the beauty of thy ornaments:

The Beloved: What shall I show ye, that ye have not seen?
Ye have seen my bracelet of Sheba's gold
that my father brought from Sidon:
Like a serpent it is shaped,
in the form of a viper:
Its head is as the most fine gold,
its crooked thighs bent like rings:
Its eyes of a coppery red
are aflame with coals of fire,
sitting in their settings:
Engraved it is by a craftsman
with bits of sapphires;
its tail is of pure-gold polished,
overlaid with smaragd stones:
All of them shine—it is wholly a delight,
this my bracelet, this my chain,
my friends, my dear ones:
Here are my circlets of gold
and all the rings of my nose,
and my earrings, ye have examined:
What else do I have, that I have not shown ye?
Ornaments, and large rings, and bracelets,
with all shapes of girdles,
hooks and beads with all the chief pendants:

The Women: Thy pearls are beautiful as drops
gleaming like dew, bright as tears:

The Beloved: Have ye seen any idols like mine?
Here is one of jacinth, of jacinth made;
carved of onyx marble,
from pieces of shell and agates,
from sandalwood, from the trunk of the pear-tree,
Astarte and hornèd Astarte:

The Women: How beautiful thine idols, beautiful beloved;
how comely are thine idols among the idols,
and this thine Astarte above all the carven images:
Who is this looking from a mantle like a bunch of
lilies,

overlaid with ivory and ebony and all sorts of
   precious stones?
She is all of polished ivory
and her eyes are sapphires;
and the hairs of her head are beaten gold,
the nipples of her breasts are ruby:

II

The Women: What is thy beloved more than another beloved,
   that so much thou dost love him?

The Beloved: My beloved is tall and powerful,
   the chosen one of his tribe:
His eyes are an eagle's eyes
that gird themselves with firebrands
lighting the dark for him like jackals:
His heart is made to be fearless,
a tiger's heart on the mountain,
his forearm is beaten iron:
Erect is my beloved,
dear friends whom I have loved,
like the sycamore in the lowland,
like the cedar of Lebanon:
His muscles are hills of chalk
based on wild plains of the desert;
like a leopard he appeareth,
excellent as panthers:

The Women: To a destroying angel of the Lord of hosts,
   we have compared him whom thy soul loveth:

The Beloved: My beloved hath a spear,
   he is clad in his apparel:
Behold, the helmet of him I have chosen—
with three rings circled, of the rings of copper:
All of them the work of a craftsman,
beaten with hammers,
one circle upon the second placed
because of the fear in battle:

His sword thirsteth for blood,
his bow panteth after flesh,
the string is not broken and hath not betrayed:
His spear is like a flash of lightning,
or the thunder of terror;
behold, it is in the back of our foe,
gleaming more than the storm,
shining more than the tempest:
His spear is made of olive wood,
its edge is of forged iron;
the eye of Death keepeth watch over its point,
in its sheath lodgeth terror:
My beloved hath a buckler carved by Chaldeans,
assuredly he doth embrace it, even make it firm,
like as a bride leaning upon her beloved:
The joints very faithfully are joined;
on his legs are glittering greaves:

III

The Beloved: My beloved hath a camel in his own stall;
a thousand pieces of silver to the camel drivers he
    gave,
in the wilderness of Paran cousins reared him:
His hairs are a blonde-grey yellow
like the sand of the desert-plains,
not to be distinguished among sands of the desert:
His legs are like a line outstretched,
thin and erect of stature,
like strings stretched on a harp:
His hooves are light and swift,
neither doth he faint or grow weary:
He passeth, and toucheth not the sand:
He passeth, and passeth away
like a shadow at noon:
Hoof-prints in the desert are not to be known,
in vain shall the enemy seek,

shall he who would ambush him look carefully:
The back of him is like a hill
and his hump like Mount Tabor,
a high hill set on the plains:
His eyes are onyx stones
in a crown of ancient kings;
his eyes are soft as a doe,
looking to the very end of the desert:
Grace and dignity is in his upright neck
that he lifteth with nobility and pride;
on it hangeth a silver crescent
whereof he boasteth in the thronging caravan:

IV

The Beloved: To the watering-troughs I went down in the
           evening,
to the well with my pitcher on my shoulder:
There I saw the mother of him my soul hath chosen,
the sister of my beloved I saw:
His mother wept and her tear was on her cheek,
sad and pale was his sister:
I asked not, that today they were thus;
I set a curb upon my mouth, I was dumb:
Philistines went up on the mountain,
Edom rushed to their prey,
ancient kings and tribes of cousins:
And the people were called together by their
           families:
My beloved, too, went forth among the army with
           banners:
And the people were smitten down, wounded they
           fell,
on the high places of the fields they bowed down:
Those that escaped returned,
and my beloved was not there:
By night on my bed I wept and slept not,

I was ashamed of my tears by day
and confounded for my sighing:
In the morning I rubbed my eyes with cold water
from the garden spring, with flowing water:
Lest I be observed by my mother, she that conceived
    me,
by my sister, and she question deeply:
I am wearied in my sighing, I bite my couch,
that my sighing go not forth in the morning:
The mother of sons is in mourning,
the husband's wife is cast down—
shall the virgins shut themselves off?

V

The Beloved: Every night I went up to the roof of my house,
I leaned upon the battlement, I looked forth:
At the beginning of the watches I greeted the
    dawn;
ah, him that my soul loveth, where art thou?
Hast thou been taken to grind before thy captors,
hast thou been sold as a slave to Philistia,
or, parched with thirst in a parched land,
didst thou stoop and fall down?
Jackals broke thy bones in pieces,
and ravens of the valley cawing
called other ravens to thy flesh:
When one flock flew away,
a second flock came after it:
Dogs clamoured, an ass brayed:
Mists before dawn in the valley
rise high as a palm tree,
leaning on rocky crags and cliffs:
The mountains of Naftali are turning blue:
The eclipsed moon is dead in the valley;
I wake, and my heart is unto him I have chosen:

VI

The Beloved: I sleep, the morning is light;
Hark! knocking at my window, my dove:
I shook like a swallow or a crane before the hunter,
like a frightened doe, I rose:
I asked not who knocked,
I inquired not:
Until that I arose to open,
my heart wanted to leave its frame,
leading me over to my beloved,
to my friend whom my soul loveth:

Saul: Open to me, my dove,
show me the vision of thee through the lattice:
For my legs drip with blood,
the palms of my hands are drops of wounds:
Six days have I been in the desert:
The arrows of Edom chased after me,
and the Philistines from the sea,
with wild beasts of the desert on every hand:
A thousand stones pierced me,
thorns and nettles cut my flesh,
the desert sand hurt my wounds:
She that conceived me, I have not yet seen:

The Beloved: Turn thou, my beloved, and flee,
for I am drunken with love;
turn thou to the mother who bore thee,
to her who conceived thee;
wipe the tear from her face,
for she doth not sleep at night,
she weepeth for thee all the day:
Until the day breath,
and the lanes of the mountains shall darken:

Odessa, 1922

ON THE BLOOD

> And I will hold as innocent their blood that I
> have not held as innocent. (Joel, 4:21)

I

Tired of mankind, the ages' legacy,
bearing a paltry and an emptied heart
bereft of strength or will, each man apart
we stumble like a horse that cannot see.

We drift like flotsam tossed by a stormy sea,
Or fetid addicts, dulled in every part;
each jealous of his fledgling, lest it start
to look towards the light, and to be free.

God's lightning rends the sky from side to side
piercing the clouds—but in our petty sight
if it appears at all, it is a spark—

thus do we stare at Genesis, squint-eyed:
in webs of mystery, rotting in the dark,
our eyes are yearning for the distant light.

II

Our eyes are yearning for the distant light:
but codes of stupid, miming apes oppress
our hearts overburdened with the pettiness
of dull and empty days, trivial and trite,

as in the days when we were young and bright
dandled by nurses, who with tenderness
re-echoed tales of vaunting wickedness,
of holy martyrs, suffering for the right.

A mushroom doctrine springs up overnight
with soldiers' curse and drivers' jest it brings
from ant-like minds, a host of verdant things

that in the scales their thousand sins outweigh,
renewing faith, a faith that passed away;
ageing, we wait the great and wondrous sight.

III

Ageing, we wait the great and wondrous sight—
O simple childish heart, who sowed that seed
of mercy, duty, love—a fatal creed—
who drew those heart-strings, sensitive and slight?

Sensitive strings! Songs there are, clear and bright—
but shamed by man, through hunger or through greed . . .
—Salvation is not near—men do not heed
mid hucksters' haggling and the cossacks' spite.

The lustres of the heavenly host abate,
on earth the mighty evil holds its sway.
Though you have saved your soul, your wound is great

yours still the vision, far from treachery . . .
When ends the dream—forever?—or a day?—
We rove and seek for creeds and mystery.

IV

We rove and seek for creeds and mystery
bald-pated or long-haired, in sombre guise
while moonstruck loons with epileptic cries
lead and mislead, and trade in ecstasy.

Dark is the fog of time and history
and like a blazing sun it blinds our eyes;
while stagnant waters whence foul vapours rise
fuse hearts to harps with monstrous alchemy.

Our soul is sick, and we are sore oppressed
with seeking, and the flame of beacons bright
bequeathed by men inspired on a great quest.

And like the chaff outside the granary
we flaunt a barren thought, we are too light,
we turn to streams, and paths of fantasy.

V

We turn to streams, and paths of fantasy . . .
With scattered crumbs and with the bread of scorn
we bow and scrape with flattering lips and fawn
on world-reformers who guide history

to magic mansions, the end of misery.
Yet when they rise—towers for midgets, shorn
of all their promise—still we hail the morn,
acclaim as promised lights the lamps we see.

Savour the pottage then, and earn its hire,
freedom for soul and body, life and light . . .
Happy the very beasts of those that buy

the magic dreams? Come tread them in the mire!
O fools, we dreamt, we who would purify,
thirsty for words of truth, limpid and bright.

VI

Thirsty for words of truth, limpid and bright,
we pay the traders' double tax and toll
with sap of guileless youth, unflawed and whole,
our warmth of spring, as with its rippling might

like pagan springs from caverns of the night . . .
Till age and weakness come, snake-like, the soul
sloughs off its skin and shelters in a hole
and through the lattice now there winks no light.

O dreams of youth, O fleeting butterflies!
You blossomed with the flowers—where do they hide?
And you were silent when the birdsong died . . .

Where are you, hero, brave of finger height?
Stumbling you fell mid vanities and lies
from trap to pit, from shadows to the night.

VII

From trap to pit, from shadows to the night
we fall, a smouldering remnant from the fire.
With a polluted blessing to inspire
glibly we praise our 'Reason'—the false light

that lulls our spirit to forget its plight
with wealth of joy and music of the lyre;
with boundaries, rules and laws do we acquire
civilized theories, crass and erudite.

Like tiny children let us be once more
a drop amid the flood, the meadows' sighs!
No search, no goal, no rule, no tyranny

as we were once in ancient days, before
we reigned over earth and light, ere we grew wise
and we were tired by seers of prophecy.

VIII

And we were tired by seers of prophecy
who longed to save the world and all mankind,
spreading their gospel, patient and resigned,
covering the world with altars like a sea.

Humble perforce, white lambs of sanctity
till they inherit—then oppress and grind
pillage and slay like ravening wolves entwined
with laurel wreaths and flaunting garlandry.

Could but the endless rivers of the blood
shed by these hungry, holy hangmen flood
the Hejaz sands and stones of Galilee

then they would bloom for all eternity
the wilderness became a grassy dell—
Cursed be the priests of idols and of Bel!

IX

Cursed be the priests of idols and of Bel
all setters-up of gods and heavenly thrones
who write their faith on parchment and on stones,
with signs and wonders, witnesses to tell.

Who offer cash for faith to those who sell
and thunderous gods and judges with harsh tones
and white and stupid fiery orbs and cones
mightily bidding joy to rise and swell.

Upon their altars too, where they revere,
they offer blood, a sacrificial toll,
bring countless thousands to the slaughter-post

all those that will not dance amid their host
the generous of heart and pure of soul
prophets of truth, and those that give them ear.

X

Prophets of truth, and those that give them ear . . .
They bear a two-edged weapon in their hand:
Love and the Truth, a wonder-working brand;
they sow their seed with prayer far and near

on brazen souls and stony hearts long sere
beguile the good, outwit the evil band,
through blood and fire they preach in every land
with zealot folly, stubborn without fear.

But falsehood reigns, and truth is hid, and spurned,
and love ferments like leaven in a bowl
and stinks on pyres where heretics are burned.

And every thinker has become a knell
though some were saved, he did not save their soul.
Let world-reformers rot in endless Hell.

XI

Let world-reformers rot in endless Hell!
Gelded of heart and tortuous of goal
with sightless mind and with forsaken soul
while their Hell gapes, of Heaven's joys they tell;

rush on their way like stupid clods, pell-mell,
shattering and rending with unending toll
the Grecian statues and the artists' scroll
they do not hear the soul of man rebel.

Until they rule and hide themselves on high
they prate of justice, sing of liberty
bold levellers who slay in sanctity;

with chains and gallows do they end their song
for those who will not bow, those who defy,
the priests of beauty and the artists' throng.

XII

The priests of beauty and the artists' throng
each pure of soul, with holy torch beside—
and if a seed of beauty he espied
it earns him pain, the lash of an envious tongue.

A Crown of briars—the guerdon of the strong.
Comes there a foe of beauty to deride?
Must Calvin have Servetus at his side?
Answer me, you who dream of tints and song!

We call for life from depths of nothingness
with myriad voices and a mystic cry
but there is no lament for us, no sigh;

we scattered tints and colours as largesse;
but of the holy purple we are clear
followers of poesy who hold her dear.

XIII

Followers of poesy who hold her dear
for you the past and future are the same
in Nile-sprung hymns that bear Ikhnaton's name
in psalms of David, welling with a tear,

a single cradle-song, that scatters cheer
on slave-born bondmaid and on high-born dame;
the weary toiler's heart shrinks as the flame
and tinted mysteries of the eve appear.

And your creation spreads a noble creed
with boundless hope, a heart afire and strong,
it gathers spark to spark and deed to deed

slowly, as gardens bloom with summer rain,
if such may be its fate, if God ordain,
they save the world with music and with song.

XIV

They save the world with music and with song
and all is one great wondrous harmony
but yet the beast of prey lurks and breaks free
in the depths of man, and bursts the binding thong.

Stripped of the wretched tatters that belong
to culture, it appears with evil glee . . .
Aeons of lofty, fine philosophy,
knowledge and faith, what have you done so long?

The flooding streams of holy purple flow
covering all the earth; man sinks in the sea . . .
our culture moulders, and the boundaries fade . . .

Does darkness conquer, or the dawn's first glow?
We peer in wonder at the twilight shade
tired of mankind, the ages' legacy.

XV

Tired of mankind, the ages' legacy,
our eyes are yearning for the distant light;
ageing, we wait the great and wondrous sight
we rove and seek for creeds of mystery.

We turn to streams, and paths of fantasy
thirsty for words of truth, limpid and bright,
from trap to pit, from shadows to the night,
they wearied us, those seers of prophecy.

Cursed be the priests of idols and of Bel
Prophets of truth and those who give them ear
Let world-reformers rot in endless Hell!

The priests of beauty and the artists' throng
followers of poesy who hold her dear
will save the world with music and with song.

                              Odessa, Berlin, 1923

ON WATCH

This night too we'll do without sleep!
The weapon we grab—that weapon keep:
pitchfork, staff, or hoe—take hold!
On watch in the field, the grain—and the cold,
we strain not to hear how the warm pulse sounds,
lest it silence the blood-thirsty desert sounds.

This night too we'll do without sleep!
For an aged mother, a father grown old,
who sanctified God with all their might,
freed the son, and blessed the daughter
to righteous war with savage men,
with spoil-hungry, blood-thirsty desert men.

This night too we'll do without sleep!
For a garden of saplings:—citrus and figs,—
beginning to sprout in a blossoming dream,
just a few seedlings in pots of clay.
And for yellow grain, on ripe stalks arrayed,
ready for the latest tractor's blade.

This night too we'll do without sleep!
For our honest cattle and our sheep,
with us here in stable and pen,
wearied by drought, just like the men;
on stalk and on furrow, like us they flood
the meagre soil with their fat and blood.

This night too we'll do without sleep!
So the wife can slumber, fearless and deep;
her heart need not fear for her man in the field,
stubborn cactus to the grasp, he will not yield—
whatever his weapon—as guard he is keeping
for the children's home—and the children sleeping.

Tel-Aviv, 1936

VULTURE! VULTURE ON YOUR MOUNTAINS

Vulture! vulture on your mountains,
   vulture on your mountains fly!
Slow and easy—for a moment—
   only floating in the sky,
floating-swimming in blue ocean,
   wakeful to the joyous hum
of heaven's heart—her wide expanse . . .
   in burning light he circles dumb.

Vulture! vulture on your mountains,
   vulture on your mountains fly!
Straight of body, heavy-limbed,
   broad of wing, and black of dye;
soars outspread (like an arrow),
   then in steady circle wheels;
from above, in rock and meadow,
   on his helpless prey he steals.

Vulture! vulture on your mountains,
   vulture on your mountains fly!
with magic touch, but wings not striking,
   swooping downward from on high.
A moment—frozen, seconds later—
   barely moving with his wings,
a slight trembling of a sudden—
   to the highest cloud he springs.

Vulture! vulture on your mountains,
   vulture on your mountains fly!
Slow and easy—for a moment—
   only floating in the sky . . .
Earth, from vulture on your mountains,
   on your face a shadow spills,
from his giant wings in passing,
   fondling the eternal hills . . .

1936

I'VE NOTHING OF MY OWN

I've nothing—not even a table—of my own!
And when at times a pale, weak moment comes,
spreading its web, at fearful evening
or silent midnight, over my brooding spirit,
then my heart, so weary of mob lies,
prays softly—no word said—
for a hand's tender touch, a heart that silent hopes,
that's dumb with you, hurt with your pain,
in all your afflictions afflicted, sharing your longings
for any hints beyond the petty sphere;

within four walls of a room that isn't yours,
which sides of stranger bodies soiled,
blurring its colours with their looks and touch,
polishing the latch, rubbing the handle smooth;
over the miserable doorway, in dust of their dregs,
telling of others' wants and alien tastes,
hang, harsh and foul, the cobweb shapes,
and the room has nothing in it which your eyes
might seek with love, no happy souvenir,
to soothe you with its sign, with hints of light or sound.

This too I know: that never shall I
build me a house, nor shall my eyes rejoice
when the eager shovel strikes rock, and the earth
bares its nakedness to make a deep foundation;
nor shall I bless each brick as it rises,
nor shall my heart sing when the strong ceiling is finished,
nor shall it be granted to me to fulfil
the commandment of building my land.

Perhaps now it wouldn't be worth it: though my hand
is still outstretched and my lamp still burns
with a bright, clear, and joyous light; yet who,
ah who, can tell if the oil in it would suffice?

No vineyard shall I plant and clear of stones,
cutting a canal for fructifying water,
for I would not plant a shoot, nor ache at its thirst,
since I have no tiny garden, nor my own plot of land,
on which to plant as my mother planted
with love and song, that youthful woman
whose vigorous beauty ripened with the joy of motherhood,—
those same modest flowers, the first of all
the crowd of the world's flowers glorified in my heart,
enslaved me by day, bewitched me in dreams.

If but I had a table! that narrow corner
in which a man is used to unite with the light
of all his essential worlds, out of a spark of life
now blurred in Infinity, an old friend's musings,
an exalted man's vision, rescued in parchment or stone;
or those blessed hours when poetry comes freely,
bursting forth like a stream from that mute song
which, cutting in the heart, must find its way out,
with all its power, for the hand to record,
flaming with joy, on pieces of paper.

I have wandered all my days, perhaps I'll wander still . . .
Property in the land is not for the wanderer,
not for me. Since this table's not my own,
then let there be placed on it a thing that's mine
completely, that stays with me where I wander,
to pour on me dream ointment of my garden,
or wrap me in the shelter of a hall my hands have builded,
that will look at me—from its pedestal—lifeless, mute,
but filled with friendship, its gaze a soft caress,—
just one thing I do want: on my table,
a single statue, carved of stone or wood.

Let the statue be made of solid basalt,
of a lump that is the blackest of the black
and consumed with the fire of creation,
like the craftsmanship of Egypt and Assyria—
a memorial for generations, and let each feature of the face
of the man to be carved in it be
cast in eternity, cast in iron and flame,
as if the man, too, were—a thing of iron and flame,
lawgiver of all the distant worlds to come,
who knew God surely face to face,
giant among earth's seers, dream of my innocent youth,
prophet of Paran's desert, of Sinai—*Moses*.

Let the statue be made of ancient copper
such as Myron moulded, and the Greek musicians
trumpeted in the islands honour to Apollo,
honour to his chief son, the first among the singers,
who peopled Olympus with crowds of pleasant gods,
blind, yet with a vision of a world so beautiful
no other eye of a seer has seen one like it since,
the man who poured out words like the music
of silver singing, now crowned with laurel bays
that never will fade, the man called *Homer*.

Let the statue be made of Pentelicus' marble,
holy marble, pregnant with the Greek gods
captured by Phidias' hand—perhaps that stone will be
clear and lovely enough to express exactly
him who dwells with silver clouds and touches the mouth of
    the deep,
reaching the truth of glory, grasping the glory of truth,
a well of wisdom and light to generations far apart,
probing the human heart and all the kingdoms of man—
brow of a peaceful god, all-seeing eye
of the prince of thought, the head of *Plato*.

Let the statue be made of Odenwald oak
and carve a *Goethe* for me with strong and gentle hand,
most splendid of men, with beauty of spirit and body.
Cut for him eyes comprehending the universe entire,
that reveal a heart which understands the visions
of dying and rising generations, embracing
the world's mighty arms, loving the riddles of suns,
interpreting the wave's meditations, telling the miracle of
    trees,
laden with all life's mysteries and speaking with dead matter,
exploring the secrets of ages in a carved bone,
a well of abundant song, to past and future wakeful.

Let the statue be made of iron, dross and dull,
yet stirring at one's touch, answering with echo's voice
like the echo which lived in his great heart, responding
to the sorrow and joy, the happiness and pain,
the love, the shame, the hatred and the mercy
of a sovereign king and lowly grave-digger,
a jester with heart of wisdom, a murderer for a price,
deceiver, glory-seeker, queen, and dissolute women,
a prince, the choicest of men, or persecuted Jew:
probing the innermost heart, the peerless one—*Shakespeare.*

Let the statue be made of Judea's stones,
hard as very flint, yet live with blood's ferment:
hard before the mighty, heart streaming forth its life,
drunk with visions, with righteousness' reign;
volcano spewing a hail of precious stones,
sorcerer of speech and flaming thought,
master of the thunders that rain from his holy mouth;
capturing all nations with magic of his wrath,
prince of the seers,—let a statue be made in the image
of the comforter of my people, *Isaiah, son of Amoz.*

Let the statue be made of ancient Indian ivory,
grown yellow, like skin tanned with the sun,
in the shape of *Astarte* for me, all veiled and robed
in a heavy cloak whose train kisses her ankle;
'none may see her and live'—each fold—a hint of life,
each wrinkle—a sigh of flame, and her lustful longings
not quite revealed in hips and thighs and breasts;
in that discipline of strength, sacred to all that live,
she appears in the glory of her beauty, to celebrate her cult—
but I—I've nothing—not even a table—of my own!

                    Jerusalem (Katamon), Tel-Aviv, 1937

BEHOLD, O EARTH

Behold, O Earth, what spendthrifts we are indeed!
Where blessing dwells, in your hidden lap, we have buried seed...
Not grains of heavy wheat, pearls of spelt with glossy coats,
no gold-sheathed barley seed, nor timid ears of oats.

Behold, O Earth, what spendthrifts we are indeed:
in you we have hid our choicest flowers, most splendid of the
    breed,
kissed by the sun's first kiss, concealing still
their grace on lovely stalks, cups of incense ready to fill.
Before they could know their noon, at innocent sorrow's core,
or drain the dew for dreams of light that their sprouting bore.

Take you the best of our sons, youth's visions of purest worth,
pure of heart, clean of hands, not soiled with filth of earth,
the fabric of their lives still weaving, with hopes of a day more
    fair,
we have none that are better than these. Have you? Then
    where?

And you shall cover all these. May the plant arise at length!
To its homeland's people sacred, in hundredfold splendour and
strength!
Blest be their offering of death, by whose glory our lives are
freed ...
Behold, O Earth, what spendthrifts we are indeed!

Tel-Aviv, 1939

CAPO VERDE

Africa ... her northern boundaries ...
in the west: the Green Cape ...
(from a geography book).

Not in vain are the dreams of a people!
Nor for naught the fables are said!
For the dream has come, and the flowers
of gold have blossomed ... the kid
is here ... and the ravishing princess ...
wholly new the skies we reach,
of a strange land, scent-bewitched ...
incantations ... and magical speech.
The kid plays in green pastures,
the princess has marvellous eyes ...
the starry sky bears me witness,
the great sea testifies!
And what was a dream of miracle,
and what was a legend long,
the hope of men imprisoned,
the key to the poet's song—
but keep you your pureness of heart,
in the innocent heart keep a place:
holy memories be your guide,
some snatches of melody's grace.

They will come—inadvertently,
and when chidings are ended all.
The miracle-song of a sudden fulfilled,
on your head the blessing will fall.

Like steel that was forged in Damascus
bright waters to right of us shone,
to the left, sea-blue, Chinese lacquer,
and a following line of loam.
That line—the helmsman told us—
was the coast of Africa there.
We turn our eyes in the morning
to the right, at grey Ocean we stare:
of a sudden appearing, upspringing,
a crowd of flying fish play,
they shoot from the sea—in a second
from our eyes they have vanished away.
It's as if a legion of soldiers
in the wave's green ambush wait,
and, presto, a thousand silver arrows
are shot at us, tiny and light.
And water and water . . . and heaven:
that reddish line again—
till suddenly, bursting before us,
the Cape of Green arose.
Capo Verde!—and the waters—
pre-equatorial—toss,
while above in the night's magic light there shine
Centaurus and the Southern Cross,
the Cape of Green! the Southern Cross!
None other! (And we, by grace
of a thin-rich volume, as children
once knew them)—now face to face.

Not in vain our dreams are spoken:
what had once been a fable scanned—
behold the Ocean . . . fish of silver . . .

foreign skies ... deep heart of the land ...
Not in vain are the dreams of a people!
Not for naught the fables are spun!
And what is believed in truly—
will *be*—my witness, the sun!
The two most beautiful legends,
the Heavens and Ocean, speak!
Inadvertently, out of despair,
in straits, and when hands are weak,
so with every myth, song of miracle!
Keep faith, in your heart, and then!
know that myth-makers carve in granite—
they *shall* be: amen, and amen!

On board the *Alsina*, 1936—Tel-Aviv, 1939

GRANDFATHER SAILS TO ODESSA

Kohelet the son of David, king in Jerusalem, expounded:
'As you cannot know the essential way of the wind,
so you cannot know where in time it comes from;
yet nevertheless, at moments, at intervals rare and infrequent,
you snatch a whisper of it, and then perhaps perceive
somewhat, the mystery of life.'
　　　　　　　　　　　　Grandfather claimed kinship
with the house of Karpiyon, known throughout the country,
and, born in the month of Adar, which is Pisces as everyone
　　knows,
he fixed into his signet, which served for a seal as well,
the figures of two small fish—that is to say, two carps.
Now Grandfather in those days had settled himself down
in a small Gentile village near Kherson called 'Empty Harbour'
(*Goláya Pristán* in Russian)—and the place 'lived up to its name':
all year round—as stated—a desolate soil and sandy,
save for green harvest time, and after wheat harvest in winter,

when there stood piled in stacks tall heaps upon heaps of
the choice of country cucumbers, gherkins of the marsh,
piled hills upon hills, all species of watermelon,
and of the melons, the sweet and the fragrant, each after its kind,
and the whole family of gourds, the large, the small, and the
    darling,
the camel gourd and the jug gourd and the tiny gourd delightful,
stalks twisting and twining, putting forth flowers of enchantment,
lovers of the sun of the steppes, glory of the orchards of Ukraine.

So Grandfather dwelt in that village, in that very Empty Harbour.
'From which you may learn'—why it was he was so fond of
    water!
Now, Grandfather had dealings with the head of the mills of
    Weinstein,
which was in 'Mother Odessa' on the Peresip—as everyone knows;
and once, being his own master—it so happened in summer—
Grandfather made up his mind to journey forth to Odessa,
and not in any steamship either, and not by any overland
route in any palanquin or any horse-drawn carriage,
but in a tiny boat, the sloop of his comrade Havrila.

This Havrila, Grandfather's chum and one of his *Hasidim*,
was a local farmer, from a line of farmers. Slow moving,
a great one for holding his tongue, for steering far away from
too much chatter at home, in the street, in the village council.
First and foremost—the chatter of his so and so, the shrew;
next from the talk and business of commune summoned to
    council;
third from every wagging tongue of every smart aleck 'barker'.
Being so fond of silence, he was naturally fond of solitude
on the sands of the clear stream, Dnieper; once he was there,
he went further and further: the very first step being
he began to sail on the river; then, once having sailed there,
he went on to make a boat with his own hands—a sloop,
one of the very smallest, the kind they used to call 'killers'.
Havrila grew wise in the river beds, where the schools of fish play,

there he would cast his line and haul out from Boristhenes
whatever the hook pulled up: carps, breams or roaches.
Always deep in thought, he never sat just fishing.
Sometimes Havrila would hazard to sail far out on the Limon
even to the tongue of Kinburn, till the desolate Isle of Berezan.
Once in a very great while Havrila and Grandfather'd meet
in a long silent session. And when the latter decided
to sail forth to Odessa, he went to Havrila's white house;
he went on the Sabbath day, and the day after Sabbath they sailed,
with the lifting of the pale dawn over the chilled river,
to take fullest advantage of the wind blowing seaward.
Provisions they took for the voyage were: one small canteen of
    water.
For Grandfather, two thebók well smoked, and one dozen hard-
boiled eggs, and a loaf of bread, and a jar of jam, and
a quarter litre of olives, with a French bread on the side,
and one roast chicken—and prayer-shawl, book, and phylacteries.
Havrila's supplies consisted of: two whole wheaten loaves
and the bitterest of cuts from the smoked fat of a bull,
and a mess of golden teran, and several white cheeses,
and a fringed pouch of Majorca, and a small jug of wine.
Till they moved off the shore and the sloop swung out into
the middle of the current, Havrila plied both oars;
the moment they reached the current, he pulled them into the
    boat,
then opened the lead rope of the mainsail, which unfurling,
and the wind blowing flush, and the good current aiding,
the boat moved straight ahead, at an easy glide.
So they sailed on the drowsy Dnieper by way of 'the throat of
    Belogrudov',
and entered the wide Limon's waters, and continued on, passing
Garibalchaya on the left, and passing Prognoysk on the right,
river banks red in the north, and river banks white in the south,
the sandy tongue of Kinburn, and Bublikov looming far off.
Then the cliff of Stanislav neared, and as they went sailing along
by way of Stanislav straits, the boat began to dance.
Farewell, farewell to you, O Isles of Verbkáh and Yanúshev!

Grandfather and Havrila sat pleasantly eating and drinking,
they were near to Berezan, when a wind blew out of the north-
west and began to sport with the vast expanse of water,
beating up ripples into waves and waves into breakers.
Suddenly white combs appeared on the crests of the waves,
and a tempest burst upon the wide sea out of nowhere.
There was nothing on all the water but the meagre boat,
and so the tempest fell upon it with all its ammunition.
Now it would race at top speed, and now it would freeze and linger,
now lift up a tremendous wave to overwhelm 'the killer',
and now dig a deep pit at its side to bury the sloop under;
suddenly drag it by main force, and as suddenly seal its
way with a wave; first fling it, then pull it back again;
powerfully snatch it from one wave to hand it to another.
The men were pummelled so hard their ribs were near to breaking,
but the mast lowered its head before every coming wave,
and came out of the tempest skipping—without oar or sail.
Three days the tempest wreaked its vengeance on 'the killer'
and then was pacified. But where were they now?
Where had the storm wind borne them? Neither of them knew:
perhaps they were in the heart of the sea, or perhaps near land . . .

Another three days becalmed—they ran out of food and water.
Weakened they lay in the boat, straining their eyes—in silence.
When behold in the south a small cloud rising and growing
into a Turkish felucca, bearing their way with all sails.
Grandfather seized his prayer-shawl and lifted it up and down,
Havrila his white kerchief, stood up and began to wave it.
The sailors caught sight of the signals and veered toward their
    direction,
took them aboard and fed them—and brought them safe to Odessa.

And it shall come to pass at the end of these troubled days,
that you shall live to be worthy of better times, and hear
of Jewish admirals serving in the navy of Argentina
under the white and blue flag! Meir, maybe, or Saul
of the Karpiyon stock. Then be advised: for sure,

they are blood cousins of mine. And if amazed you inquire:
'Sons and grandsons of merchants—what's a navy to them, and
   what water?
And how came their father to leave them admiral's epaulets?'
This is the reason why: Because he was born in a small
harbour—Empty Harbour, that is, at the mouth of the Dnieper,
and his grandfather voyaged himself—from near Kherson to
   Odessa—
not in a vessel under steam, and not in a ship under sails,
but in a very small sloop—to be accurate, a 'killer'—
'through the wet path of the waters', in the words of Homer the
   Greek.
And maybe—God only knows!—in the veins of his father's fathers
there beat one drop in sixty of the same spirit that was
with the sons of your people of old on the shore of Etzion Geber,
chanters of sea chanteys in the beach huts of Zebulon
who went down to the sea in ships—Phoenician galleys to Ophir—
a very long voyage it was, very very long indeed . . . .
Who knows the way of the wind, and what she brings in her
   wings?
For those same marvellous sparks from the ancient powerful days,
shepherds and herdsmen and smiths who were scribes, and
   physicians,
who became in the course of time, and in altered surroundings,
judges, kings, and prophets, teachers and pillars of the law,
straying Messiahs and poets and kabbalist visionaries,
exegetes irate-eyed, and founders of the great academies,
Hasidic luminaries and all who suffered the pain of their people,
men of wisdom and men of virtue and the great intercessors—
'Generation of Samuel—Samuel; generation of Jeptha—Jeptha'—
and all those holy sparks whose light was never found worthy
to shine in the great world, and so expired from lack of
air in the ghetto straits and in the great pitchblackness—
those marvellous sparks are yet to be revealed again,
shall again take fire, be lights to this poor people,
to all men—great lights! 'By Israel's Eternal!'

                          1941

BALLAD OF THE WOLF

A band of Crusaders wanders
    through cities, spreading fear:
they've butchered men in Aachen,
    they'll butcher soon in Trier.

They're ready for the slaughter:
    while the church-bell rings,
righteous and rabble together
    divide the loot it brings.

In a heap they leave the victims,
    their slaughtered bodies bared;—
the city-folk must bury them
    (no single soul was spared).

The man of the Cross can't be bothered:
    for, busy every day,
he must sing to the man of Nazareth,
    fast, and butcher, and pray.

But a wolf that was Heaven-fearing
    hard-by was living then,
in his cave deep in the thicket
    of a cool and shady glen.

Before the hound could get there,
    or raven swoop for its share,
the wolf to the valley of slaughter went,
    and he worked quickly there.

Finding a skull that, shattered,
    a living soul still bore,
which for death was pleading,—
    into its heart he tore.

Finding a trampled baby
    hungry for the breast,
and kicking still,—he at once
    choked her, and gave her rest.

Finding a man expiring,
    whom a faulty knife had slain,—
he gnawed the windpipe clean and bare—
    an end to the terrible pain.

Finding a womb split open,
    that still to be labouring seemed,—
he tore the part that was living,
    and torture was redeemed.

Then Rabbi Yuzpha saw him,
    who, one whole day and more,
arms chopped and body legless,
    had lain there, bleeding sore.

He saw him, blessed him, stretching
    his neck to him in need:
'Blessed among wolves of the evening!
    Blessèd who does His deed!

'The tenth generation—will see it,
    you who our pain released
and gave us death's redemption
    blessèd will be, O beast!

'Your seed shall not cease in this land
    but still shall live—and then
shall become a prince of killers,
    be wolves instead of men!'

Generations die, are established,
  the days roll on their way,
and Rabbi Yuzpha's blessing
  we see fulfilled today.

Man has turned prince of killers,
  become a wolf instead,
and the seed of the wolf is vanished,
  is dead, is dead, is dead . . .

                      Tel-Aviv, 1942

NOTES TO THE POEMS

p. 95 'I Believe': Published in *The Reflex*, VI, No. 4, September, 1935.

p. 96 'Plant Strange to Your People': Published in *The Jewish Quarterly*, London, Autumn, 1955, p. 17. Written as if to a woman; but, since the 'plant' seems descriptive of the poet himself, many critics interpret the second person here as his Muse.

p. 97 'Before a Statue of Apollo': Published in *The Chicago Jewish Forum*, Spring, 1950, pp. 182–3, and in *A Little Treasury of World Poetry* (ed. H. Creekmore), New York, Scribner's, 1952, pp. 80–1.

p. 98 'Tavria': Thus in Hebrew. Also spelled 'Taurida' and 'Tavrida'.

'*shoḥeṭ*': Man qualified to perform the ritual slaughter of animals.

Ha-Zefirah: A Hebrew weekly and then daily published intermittently in Warsaw (1862–1927). The first of its kind in Poland, an organ of the Haskalah tendency.

p. 99 'Bilivirka': Slightly modified version of Byelozorka (cf. Tavria).

p. 100 '*mohel*': Man qualified to perform the rite of circumcision. The functions of *shoḥeṭ* and *mohel* were frequently performed by the same man.

p. 101 'Kondrat', 'Godel', 'Danila': A jest at the habit of adopting gentile names which have nothing in common with their Jewish originals, except perhaps for a single consonant (as a 'Moses' in America will become a 'Milton').

p. 102 'on thigh and on hip': Judges, 15:8.

p. 103 'Bakhchi-Saray': see the narrative poem by A. Pushkin, 'The Fountain of Bakhchi-Saray'.

p. 104 'Chazarim': A people of Turkish origin who lived in southern Russia in the early Middle Ages and adopted the Jewish religion; expelled by the Russians in the tenth–eleventh centuries.

'the Ninth of Av': *Tish'a B'Av* in Hebrew. Eliakim remembers the day of the destruction of the Temple.

p. 105 'Ahad Ha'am': 'One of the People', pen-name of Asher Ginsberg (1856–1927), writer and founder of so-called 'cultural Zionism', whose essays are classics of modern Hebrew literature.

p. 106 'Circumcision': For background to this section of the poem, see the article 'Circumcision' in *The Jewish Encyclopedia* (New York, 1903, Vol. IV).

'*melammed*': A Hebrew teacher; in Jewish folklore, usually poor and unworldly. Shmerel represents a new type ('they knew he was clever, though a *melammed*').

p. 107 'shabos-goy': A Yiddish phrase signifying a 'Sabbath-Gentile', namely one who performed necessary tasks forbidden to Jews on the Sabbath, as described in the text.

'Montefiore and Hirsch': Prominent Jewish philanthropists. Sir Moses Montefiore (1784–1885), was particularly interested in helping the Jews settle in Palestine. Baron Maurice de Hirsch (1831–1896) was the founder of the Jewish Colonization Association (ICA), the spearhead for colonization efforts in the Argentine. After their deaths, the execution of their wills aroused fierce disputes.

p. 108 '*kvatter*': One of the two individuals honoured by being allowed to assist the *mohel* as he performs the circumcision.

p. 109 '*Shechinah*': The holy, in-dwelling presence of God.

'a holy silence reigned ... ': With excellent tact, the poet omits any description of the actual operation by the *mohel*.

'*chala*': White bread, customary for holidays and festive occasions.

p. 110 'whiskey': In the original, 'monopolka', a Russian word used for alcoholic liquors, which were held as a 'monopoly' by the Tsarist governments.

'To Life!': The familiar Jewish toast: *Le-Ḥayyim!*

'the millstones': i.e., the molar teeth (the same word in Hebrew).

'*gefilte*': 'stuffed', in Yiddish.

p. 111 'Carmel': World-famous wines, from the cellars established with the help of Baron Edmond de Rothschild (1845–1934) in Rishon Le-Zion and Zichron Yaakov.

'the ICA oppression': Referring to the period when there were labour-disputes between the workers in Rishon and Zichron and the administrators of those colonies, which, after 1899, were managed by the Jewish Colonization Association founded by Baron de Hirsch.

p. 112 *'ganef'*: from the Hebrew, Yiddish for 'thief'; used in both English and American slang.

'Litvak': A Lithuanian. This form of the word, when used by non-Lithuanians, often carries with it a note of contempt. 'two sets of *tefillin*': See below, note to p. 116. Lithuanian Jews were pious—hence the two sets of phylacteries—when they did not go to the other extreme of radicalism; but the series of 'doubles' here (names, *tefillin*, wives) are all intended to lead up to the last. Since Lithuania, though a seat of Jewish learning, was not a prosperous country, many a Lithuanian *melammed* was forced to travel abroad in search of employment, usually returning to his family for the holidays—somewhat like a sailor. Thus, there were many 'actual cases' to justify Shebsili's dig.

p. 113 *'Haggadah'*: The text of the ritual for the Passover Seder. Shmerel's question refers to the famous *Had Gadya* song with which the Seder concludes—a sort of 'House That Jack Built' theme, in which a kid is eaten by a cat; a cat by a dog; and so on through a stick, the fire, the water, the ox, the slaughterer, the Angel of Death, and the Holy One, blessed be He. . . .

'*kreplach*': Yiddish: pieces of dough filled with meat or cheese.

p. 114 'Baruch of Mayence': Published in *Poet Lore*, Summer, 1948, pp. 139–61; also fragments in Jewish Education Committee booklet, p. 15 and *Furrows*, September, 1947, pp. 24–5.

This masterpiece of Tschernichowsky's early period was first printed in 1902 and helped firmly establish his youthful reputation. Its historic kernel was taken from Jewish accounts of the massacres of the First Crusades, according to which Isaac Ben David and Uri of Mayence, a city on the Rhine, after forced baptism, returned to that city; the former, killing his two daughters and setting fire to his home, perished in the flames with his companion. The poet's chief deviation from his source is that Baruch sets fire to the monastery, making the story one of revenge instead of martyrdom; also, the change of name to Baruch (Blessed) is an ironical commentary.

The poem begins at the end of the story, which unfolds gradually through the events of three days. Baruch does not tell his story consecutively but frequently refers to memories of a happier past.

The metres of the original have been preserved in the translation. It is worth noting that an early version of sections 4–8 was published in the first volume of *Visions and Melodies*, showing that part at least of the conception had antedated 1898.

p. 116 Bar-Miẓvah': A ceremony performed at the age of 13 marking the Jewish boy's assumption of adult status.

'*tefillin*': Phylacteries, worn on the arm and forehead during prayer; they are bound on the arm with a leather strap, as described in the poem.

'Betroth thee unto Me . . .' *Hosea*, 2:21–2. Part of the prayer recited while putting on the *tefillin*.

p. 124 'Pour out Thy wrath . . .': Adapted from the famous prayer, included in the *Haggadah* of Passover, from Psalms 79:6.

p. 134 'The Broken Spoon': Translation by L. Bernard. The poem is the product of Tschernichowsky's brief sojourn in prison as a 'political prisoner'. See above p. 20.

p. 139 'She-Pilgrim': Translation by L. V. Snowman, under the title 'Festival Pilgrim' in *Tchernichovski and his Poetry with Renderings from the Hebrew*, London, 1929.

p. 140 'Death of Tammuz': Compare Tschernichowsky's note to a *Lament for Tammuz*, which he translated from the Babylonian (via German) into Hebrew: 'Tammuz is the Adonis of the Greeks, whose cult was a very important one: he was the god of the sun, the god of fertility and growth, the young mate of Ashtoreth. Every year he descends to Sheol, and then the whole creation perishes: his mother, sister, and wife mourn for him, till he returns to earth in the Spring.'

p. 141 'Asherah': 'A sacred piece of wood, . . . sometimes a tree or stump of a tree, with or without carvings, found always beside the altar in a Canaanitish high place, and usually considered to be a survival of an earlier tree worship.' (Webster's New International Dictionary, 1931.)

p. 142 'To the Sun': This version of a 'cycle' of sonnets (the Hebrew word is *klil*, meaning 'wreath' or 'crown', with an adjectival sense implying wholeness, completeness, perfection) is an attempt to render, however imperfectly, this rare poetic form into English.

In the Introduction to his 'Little Book of Sonnets' (Jerusalem–Berlin, 1922), Tschernichowsky claimed that 'To the

Sun' was the first such cycle in Hebrew, and mentioned two Russian poets who had written cycles, Constantine Balmont and Vyacheslav Ivanov.

Otherwise known as the crown or corona of sonnets, or the sonnet-garland, the cycle originated in thirteenth-century Italy. It was imitated by the Russian Symbolist poets at the beginning of the twentieth century, its exponents including V. Brjusov, M. Voloshin and V. Ivanov—the latter in *Cor Ardens* and *Chelovek* (see also O. Deschartes' article in *Oxford Slavonic Papers* V, 1954, pp. 56–7). Tschernichowsky uses precisely this form, in which the fifteenth and 'master' sonnet, presumably written first, contains the thematic and compositional key to the preceding fourteen. Each of its lines in turn provides both the closing line of one sonnet and the opening line of the next, the fourteenth sonnet ending with the first line of the completed cycle. The effect is that of a unified, but very complex, idea being unfolded with deliberate care (not incompatible with passion, of course) to an inevitable conclusion.

Some of the special formal qualities of the poem in the original Hebrew will be realized if the English reader keeps in mind that the original sonnets all follow the complex rhyme-scheme of the Italian or Petrarchan type; and that, blessed with the profusion of rhymes which the Hebrew language makes possible, the poet also maintained a constant alternation of masculine and feminine rhymes.

Confronted with a form so perfect and so complete, our translation has adopted many compromises. Rhyme has been attempted only in Sonnet XV, which, like the original concluding sonnet, had, of course, to be written (translated) first. For the rest, an attempt has been made to approximate the original rhythm, which is an iambic hexameter, with a strong caesura after the third foot. The original rhyme schemes are suggested by the fashion in which the lines are divided and indented, which is the same style of printing adopted by Tschernichowsky for his Hebrew. This version was originally published in *Israel Argosy*, 3, ed. I. Halevy-Levin, Jerusalem, 1954, pp. 152–75. For a rhymed translation by Isaac Schwartz see *Midstream*, Vol. XII, No. 2, February, 1966. 'Sukkah, Ch. V, Mishnah 4': Referring to Ezekiel 8:16.

'mallow': 'Mauve, mallow, Malve (Shabbat, 35. "The name of a flower which bows down and leans toward the sun." M. Schulbaum, *General Dictionary*).' (Tschernichowsky's note.)

p. 145 'with scalpel sharp in my hand': Tschernichowsky practised surgery.

p. 146 'the elephant tree': Klausner interprets this as 'the largest of the trees'.

p. 147 'the Mount of Mounts': Hebrew: *hor ha-har*. Usually interpreted as a mountain on the border of Edom, 'the next stopping-place after Kadesh of the children of Israel during their wanderings in the wilderness; famous as the scene of Aaron's death' (*The Jewish Encyclopedia;* see Numbers 20: 22–9). But the poet is probably using this superlative form to refer to Mount Sinai, since 'a giant with fiery law!' could only be Moses—or, at least, this is how we prefer to interpret *hor ha-har*.

'Perun': 'The Slavic god' (Tschernichowsky's note). The Thunderer, with whom is identified Svarog, god of heaven.

p. 149 'Ashéroth': see note, p. 140.

p. 151 'There Was a King in Israel': The first two lines are quoted faithfully from Moses' blessing to the children of Israel before his death (Deuteronomy 33:5).

p. 152 'This Be Our Revenge': Among the works inspired by pogroms the poet witnessed in 1919. The Ukrainian nationalists under Petlura looked upon pillage and rape as a means of paying the soldiers, and were later followed by the Polish army. The official Soviet government finally put a stop to it, but neither Petlura nor his compatriot Denikin was ever punished.

Published in *The Voice*, Order Sons of Zion, November, 1943. On the problem of revenge in Tschernichowsky, see S. J. Kahn 'Tschernichowsky's Prophecies of Revenge', *Opinion*, August, 1947, pp. 6–7.

p. 155 'The Grave': Translation by L. V. Snowman.

p. 156 'And there ran a man ... ': This is the poet's own motto. The full text of Rashi is 'That was Saul who snatched the tables from the hand of Goliath and fled.'

The assigning of lines—to The Women, The Beloved, and Saul—is not in the text. It has been added, as in some printings of 'The Song of Songs', not in order to impose a dramatic

structure on the poem, but as a substitute for the clear varia-
tions of number and gender, natural in the inflected Hebrew,
but impossible in English. No attempt has been made—except
in the language itself, which attempts to follow that of the
King James Bible—to indicate fully the poet's 'play' with his
biblical sources.

p. 163 'On the Blood': Published in a previous version in *Sifrut 2*,
London, 1956, pp. 29–35.

    L. Bernard's translation achieves the remarkable *tour de
force* of remaining faithful to the original rhyme-scheme, but
changes the rhythm, which is a dactylic tetrameter, to an
iambic pentameter. The reader may be interested in com-
paring S. J. Kahn's version of Sonnet XV (published in *Here
and Now*, Jerusalem, 13 October 1955, p. 17):

> Weary of mankind and the gifts of the ages
>   our failing eyes peer to lights from afar;
>   we grow old, as we wait for the miracle great.
> We search the mysteries of all the sacred pages.

> To imagination we turn, to the sources aspiring,
>   athirst for words of pure truth we can keep.
>   From trap to pit, from depths to the deep,
> the prophets deceive, the gospellers are tiring.

>   Accursed be the priests of Sun-gods and Bel!
> And the prophets of truth and all the conformers!
> An eternal curse on the names of reformers!

>   But priests of beauty and art will never fail,
> masters of the Muse, in her mysteries strong,
> to redeem the world with melody and song.

p. 168 'Must Calvin have Servetus ..': Michael Servetus (1511–53),
Spanish physician and theologian, was arraigned for blas-
phemy, condemned, and burned at the stake, at the instance
of John Calvin (1509–64), himself one of the great leaders of
the Protestant Reformation.

p. 170 'On Watch': Published in 'English Magazine', *The Day* (a
Yiddish newspaper), 28 December 1947. Written at the
beginning of the period of intensified Arab attacks, from
1936 to 1939.

p. 172 'Vulture! ... ': Published in *Here and Now*, 14 September 1955, p. 18. See an unrhymed version and discussion in S. Halkin, *Modern Hebrew Literature*, pp. 151–2.

p. 173 'I've Nothing of My Own': Published in the *Jewish Frontier*, October, 1948, pp. 40–1. When this poem was written, Tschernichowsky's family was living in a furnished apartment in the Katamon district of Jerusalem.

p. 175 'Myron': Greek sculptor.
'Pentelicus': Mountain, north-east of Athens, famous for its marble quarries.

p. 177 'Behold, O Earth': Published in *Pioneer*, October–November, 1950, p. 26.

p. 178 'Capo Verde': The title is given in Latin letters.

p. 180 'Grandfather Sails to Odessa': Translation by Jacob Sloan, published in *Commentary*, January, 1948, pp. 559–62.

p. 182 'thebok': A kind of bream, from the Don River.

p. 185 'Ballad of The Wolf': From a group of seven ballads entitled 'Ballads of Worms' written within a few months in 1942. Worms is a city on the Rhine, Germany. The poet's notes refer to historical Jewish persecutions during the thirteenth and fourteeth centuries, including the period of the Black Death, when the congregation of Worms (300 souls) was destroyed (1349).
'Trier': A city on the Moselle River. The crusaders destroyed the congregation in 1096, month of Sivan. (Tschernichowsky's note.)

BIBLIOGRAPHICAL NOTE

TWENTY-FIVE years have elapsed since the death of Saul Tschernichowsky. There is still no complete edition of his works. Even
the ten-volume edition, published between 1929 and 1934, does
not contain all his stories or all his translations or even all his
poems up to that time. Nor does it include his feuilletons and his
critical articles, his monograph on Immanuel of Rome, his children's
poems and children's stories. A new multivolume edition of Tschernichowsky's poetry and prose is a real desideratum.

Until 1966, the best edition of Tschernichowsky's poems was the
one-volume edition published by Schocken in 1937 and republished
several times. It was the most comprehensive, almost complete collection of his poetry; only the children's poems were excluded. In
1966 a two-volume edition of Tschernichowsky's poetry was published by Dvir. The poems were arranged—not too felicitously—
in two genre groups. Mistakes of previous editions have been eliminated.

Tschernichowsky's children's poems are accessible, although
not in their entirety, in two small volumes published by Dvir, Tel-
Aviv–Berlin, 1922 under the title *He-Ḥalil* (The Flute) and by
Yavneh, Tel-Aviv, 1946 under the title *Shirim le-Yeladim* (*Children's
Poems*). Illustrations for both volumes were furnished by the well-
known Jewish artist, Nahum Gutman. Two collections of children's
poems were published in 1936: *Goren-Shirim Nibḥarim le-Yalde
Yisrael le-Yobel ha-Shishim Shel ha-Meshorer* (*Barn—Selected Poems
for Jewish Children—for the Sixtieth Anniversary of the Poet*, Tel-Aviv,
1936), *Shire S. Tschernichowsky le-Aḥaw ha-Ẓe'irim* (*Poems of Saul
Tschernichowsky for his Younger Brethren*, Riga, 1936).

The critical articles and feuilletons are scattered in many periodicals. The series entitled *Odessa she-Metah* (Odessa That Died)
appeared in the seventh volume of his collected writings, Tel-Aviv,
1932, pp. 15–225. It is especially valuable for an appraisal of Tschernichowsky's school years in the city which was a centre of Jewish
culture. It also throws light on minor literary figures and scholars in

Odessa. For reference to works treating the major figures see Chapter V, note 11.

The children's tales are accessible in a volume called *Asher Hayah we-lo-Hayah* (What Was and What Was Not). It appeared under the imprint of Yavneh in 1942 and it was illustrated by Nahum Gutman.

The casual drawings by Tschernichowsky appeared in *Mo'znayim* XVII, November, 1963. In that issue the artist and illustrator of Tschernichowsky's poems for children, Nahum Gutman as well as the poet Abraham Braudes published brief evaluations of Tschernichowsky's drawings. Unpublished material is hard to come by: some manuscripts are available in the Israeli literary archives, *Genazim*, and in the National and University Library of Jerusalem. Some are in private hands. Not a single volume of letters has appeared so far.

The most valuable work on Tschernichowsky was written by J. Klausner. His book *Sha'ul Tschernichowsky: Ha-Adam we-ha Meshorer* (Saul Tschernichowsky: The Man and The Poet) appeared in Jerusalem in 1947, published by the Hebrew University Press Association. It is a biography, a commentary on individual poems and a critical analysis of his work. It is based on the biographical and evaluative articles which appeared in Klausner's book *Yozerim u-Bonim III* (Creators and Builders III), published by Dvir in Tel-Aviv in 1929.

Joseph Lichtenbaum's book *Sha'ul Tschernichowsky: Toldotaw we-Yezirato* (Saul Tschernichowsky: His Life and His Work) appeared in Jerusalem in 1946. In its biographical section it is based on Klausner's articles; in its evaluative section it maintains a conservative, descriptive approach to the work of the poet. It lists a large number of musical settings of Tschernichowsky's poems.

Jacob Fichmann published a fine study on Tschernichowsky in *Ammat Ha-Binyan* (The Builder's Instrument) which deals with the major Hebrew writers of Odessa. It appeared in Jerusalem in 1951.

Yom-Tov Hellman's *Perakim le-Shire Sha'ul Tschernichowsky* (Chapters to the Poems of Saul Tschernichowsky) contains many fine insights. It was published in Jerusalem in 1956.

Baruch Kurzweil's study *Bialik we-Tschernichowsky* (Bialik and Tschernichowsky) was published by Schocken Publishing House Ltd., Tel-Aviv, 1960, third expanded edition, 1967. It is, in the main, a collection of essays, written over a period of 15 years, on the two major poets of the Hebrew literary renaissance. They suffer from the critic's doctrinaire attitude toward modern Hebrew literature. His theory, enunciated in a previous book *Sifrutenu ha-Ḥadashah-Hemshek O Mahapekah* (Our Modern Literature-Continuity or Revolution), maintains that modern Hebrew literature broke with the past which was sacral in character: and this break inaugurated a new, superficial epoch. 'What gives direction to our modern literature is the final parting of that profane literature from its sacral sources.'[1] The poetry of Bialik is a continuous struggle with the possibilities of return to traditional values—to nature, to a reborn people, to one's self. The poetry of Tschernichowsky, in the view of Kurzweil, is also—thematically at least—a poetry of return. But Bialik gropes his way toward a traditional, religious return; Tschernichowsky's poetry, in stark opposition to diaspora values, struggles with a return to the archaic and the mythological. The motif of return is the meeting point of two poets who are not as dissimilar as they were thought to be in the past decades.[2]

A. Sha'anan, *Ha-Sifrut ha-'Ibrit ha-Ḥadashah li-Zeramehah* (Currents in Modern Hebrew Literature) the first three volumes of which appeared in Israel in 1962, devotes a long chapter to Tschernichowsky in the third volume (pp. 237–311). It re-evaluates the work of Tschernichowsky and sheds new light on the idylls.

All anthologies of modern Hebrew poetry carry Tschernichowsky's poems. Hundreds of articles have been written about Tschernichowsky during his lifetime and since his death. On special occasions—on his fiftieth and sixtieth anniversaries—entire sections of the foremost Hebrew periodicals were devoted to his life and work.

Of the important periodicals which have allotted much space to the anniversaries of Tschernichowsky, the following should be mentioned: *Ha-Shiloaḥ* XXXV,[2] August, 1918. The entire issue is

1. Baruch Kurzweil, *Bialik we-Tschernichowsky*, p. XIV.   2. *Ibid.*, p. XII.

called *Ḥoberet Tschernichowsky* (Tschernichowsky Issue); *Bitzaron*, November, 1943—Tschernichowsky issue; *Mo'znayim* 1935—Sixtieth Anniversary Issue; *Mo'znayim*, November, 1963—in commemoration of the twentieth anniversary of the death of the poet; *Gilyonot*, 1935—Sixtieth Anniversary Issue; *Ha-Rofe' ha-'Ibri—The Hebrew Medical Journal*, New York, 1944: the entire issue is dedicated to appraisals of the work of Saul Tschernichowsky; also part of *Ha-Rofe' ha-'Ibri*, 1964, with bilingual articles—in Hebrew and in English—on the poet and reprints of articles from the 1944 issue.

The most recent bibliography of Saul Tschernichowsky's writings and a selection of articles on him has been edited by Y. Barzillai, Genazim, Tel-Aviv, 1966.

Translations from Tschernichowsky's works into English are available in numerous anthologies. Frequently, they are also used to illustrate evaluative essays on his poetry. Most essays and comments on Tschernichowsky in English, however, reveal the curious fact that appreciation of his work rarely rises above biographical information and generalized evaluation.

The following bibliography on Tschernichowsky in English, although by no means exhaustive, may guide the reader to a greater awareness of his work:

R. Alter, 'The Kidnapping of Bialik and Tschernichowsky', *Midstream*, June, 1964, pp. 27–35; *idem*, Translations of three poems of Saul Tschernichowsky with comments in *The Modern Hebrew Poem Itself*, ed. Stanley Burnshaw, T. Carmi, Ezra Spicehandler, New York, Chicago, San Francisco, 1965, pp. 35–47; Nathan and Marynn Ausubel, *A Treasury of Jewish Poetry from Biblical Times to the Present*, New York, 1957, pp. 72, 75, 195, 227, 228, 390; Harry Herzl Fein, *A Harvest of Hebrew Verse*, Boston, 1934, pp. 111–22; *idem*, *Titans of Hebrew Verse*, Boston, 1936, pp. 61–90; *idem*, *Gems of Hebrew Verse*, Boston, 1940, pp. 21, 22, 23, 52, 53, 54, 68, 69, 85, 113; E. Fleg, *The Jewish Anthology*, translated by Maurice Samuel, New York, 1925; Joseph Leftwich, *Yisroel*, New York, 1963, pp. 683–9; Ruth Finer Mintz, *Modern Hebrew Poetry*, a bilingual anthology, Berkeley and Los Angeles, 1966, pp. 38–73; D. Patterson, 'Saul Tchernichovsky' in *Sifrut 2*, London, 1956, pp. 14–28; Philip M.

Raskin, *Anthology of Modern Jewish Poetry*, New York, 1927, pp. 155–157; Menachem Ribalow, *The Flowering of Modern Hebrew Literature*, ed. and tr. by Judah Nadich, New York, 1959, pp. 88–122; *A Golden Treasury of Jewish Literature*, ed. Leo W. Schwartz, Philadelphia, 1946, pp. 619–25; *The Menorah Treasury*, ed. Leo. W. Schwartz, Philadelphia, 1964, pp. 681–2; Eisig Silberschlag, 'Saul Tschernichowsky: Poet of Myths', *Commentary I*, New York, 1946, pp. 46–57; *idem*, 'Tschernichowsky and Homer', *Proceedings of the American Academy of Jewish Research* XIV, New York, 1944, pp. 253–65; L. V. Snowman, *Tchernichovski and his Poetry with Renderings from the Hebrew*, London, 1929; S. Spiegel, *Hebrew Reborn*, New York, 1930, pp. 319–29, 423–35; Saul Tschernichowsky, 'To The Sun', a sonnet sequence translated by Isaac Schwartz, *Midstream*, February, 1966; M. Waxman, *A History of Jewish Literature* IV, 1941, pp. 259–81. In the two-volume *Anthology of Modern Hebrew Poetry* (Institute for the Translation of Hebrew Literature and Hebrew Universities Press), Jerusalem, 1966, Tschernichowsky's poems appear on pages 57–93 of the first volume.

For general background reading, the following works in English will be found useful:

H. BAVLI, 'The Modern Renaissance of Hebrew Literature', in *The Jews: Their History, Culture and Religion*, Philadelphia, 1949.

B. BENSHALOM, *Hebrew Literature Between the Two Wars*, Jerusalem, 1953.

S. HALKIN, *Modern Hebrew Literature, Trends and Values*, New York, 1950.

J. L. LANDAU, *Short Lectures on Modern Hebrew Literature*, London, 1938.

D. PATTERSON, *Abraham Mapu*, London, 1964.

D. PATTERSON, *The Hebrew Novel in Czarist Russia*, Edinburgh, 1964.

J. S. RAISIN, *The Haskalah Movement in Russia*, Philadelphia, 1913.

M. RIBALOW, *The Flowering of Modern Hebrew Literature*, New York and London, 1959.

E. SILBERSCHLAG, *Hebrew Literature: An Evaluation*, New York, 1959.

N. SLOUSCHZ, *The Renascence of Hebrew Literature*, Philadelphia, 1909.

S. SPIEGEL, *Hebrew Reborn*, London, 1931.

R. WALLENROD, *The Literature of Modern Israel*, New York and London, 1956.

M. WAXMAN, *A History of Jewish Literature*, New York, Vols. 3 and 4, rev. ed., 1960.

INDEX OF POEMS: HEBREW TITLES

INDEX OF POEMS: ENGLISH TITLES

GENERAL INDEX

Abinadab, 55
Agrippa I, 46
Aguilar, Grace, 7
Ahad Ha'am, 9, 15, 188
Albright, W. F., 50
Almanzi, Joseph, 59
Alter, R., 199
Altmann, Alexander, 11
Amir, Anda Pinkerfeld, 71
Anacreon, IX, 26, 87
Anguillara, Giovanni Andrea dell', 44
Antisemitism, 62
Aristotle, 41, 42, 48
Arlozorov, 33
Arnold, Matthew, 85
Astarte, 40, 45, 57
Athenaeus, 49
Auden, W. H., 36
Ausubel, Nathan, 199
Ausubel, Marynn, 199
Azriel, 67

Bader, Gershom, 11
Bahat, Jacob, 54
Balmont, C., 192
Barzillai, Y., 199
Baudelaire, 36
Bavli, H., 200
Bel, 22
Ben Avigdor, 13
Ben Gutman, 89
Benshalom, Benzion, 49, 58, 200
Ben-Zion, S., 44
Bérard, V., 50

Berdyczewski, 20, 22, 37, 42, 53, 91
Bernard, L., 191, 194
Bialik, Hayyim Nahman, IX, 6, 8, 9, 11, 14, 20, 21, 28, 30, 33, 36, 47, 55, 58, 62, 71, 75, 92, 198
Biblical References: Genesis 18:1, 20; 25:27, 89; Exodus 15:1–18, 51; Numbers 13:23, 56; 33:35–6, 5; Deuteronomy 2:8, 5; 1 Samuel 4:12, 56; 28:7–25, 53; 31:11–13, 56; 2 Samuel 17:15, 55; 1 Kings 9:26; 22:49, 5; Isaiah 34:13–14, 40; 13:21, 40; Ezekiel 8:16, 41, 61; Proverbs 31:31, 50; 1 Chronicles 17:13, 55; 10:12, 56; 2 Chronicles 8:17; 20:36, 5
Bilu, 91
Bosak, Meir, 69
Brainin, Reuben, 12, 13, 14
Braudes, Abraham, 197
Brjusov, V., 192
Bunin, Ivan, 83
Burns, 12, 65, 66, 83
Burnshaw, Stanley, 199

Callinus of Ephesus, 43
Calvin, J., 194
Campbell, J. F., 65
Carmi, T., 199
Child, Francis James, 65
Coffin, Tristram P., 65
Cohen, Jacob, 38
Cohen, Shalom, 49
Coleridge, 65
Croiset, M., 48

Tschernichowsky, Saul: Works: Ḥezyonot u-Manginot (Visions and
Melodies) 12, 13, 15, 18, 63, 65,
66, 191; Shirim, 66; Shirim Ḥadashim, 27; Re'i Adamah, 34, 88;
The Schocken edition of his poems:
37, 38, 43, 46, 59, 60, 63, 64, 65, 68,
73, 80, 87, 196; The Dvir edition
of his poems, 196; Kitbe Shaul
Tschernichowsky (Collected Works
of Saul Tschernichowsky) 9, 13,
24, 26, 70, 74, 77, 78, 86, 87, 196;
Play: Bar-Kohba, 28, 72–5; Stories:
13, 24, 26, 46, 47, 75–9;
Children's Poems and Tales, 27,
34, 70–72, 196–7; Science: 23, 79–
82; Translations by Tschernichowsky, 22, 27, 28, 31, 41, 45,
60, 66, 75, 83–8; Translations of
Tschernichowsky into English,
93–187, 199–200

Ugarit, 40
Uriah the Hittite, 8, 52

Verne, 8
Virgil, 44
Voloshin, M., 192
Voss, Johann Heinrich, 24

Wallenrod, R., 201
Waxman, M., 200, 201
Wessely, 49
Williams, William Carlos, 79
Witt, Marion, 66
Wolfson, H. A., 42, 90
Wordsworth, 65

Yarden, Dov, 29
Yeats, William Butler, 48, 66

Zedekiah, 37
Zemah, Nahum, 28
Zionism, 38, 62